The Slave Streets of LIVERPOOL

David Hearn

Edited by Richard Jackson

For the one and a half million men, women and children carried on Liverpool ships from their homes in Africa to lives of toil and misery in the Americas.

Acknowledgments

Richard, the other half of the Dusty Teapot Company CIC, who edited, stitched this all together and assembled my very speedy writing into something that is presentable.

Helen, who listens to my endless stories and, almost always, manages to feign interest.

About the Author

After a career of 35 years in banking and finance David took a BA in History at Liverpool John Moores University and Edge Hill University before taking his Masters in International Slavery Studies at the University of Liverpool.

David is now one half of The Dusty Teapot Company CIC which promotes, preserves and protects the heritage and culture of Merseyside where he is very active on Twitter (@thedustyteapot) and on their website www.dustyteapot.co.uk

He is a public speaker and has broadcast on radio and television (his appearance on Channel 5 should be around the same time as publication of this book!).

"Almost every man in Liverpool is a merchant; the attractive African meteor has so dazzled their ideas, that almost every order of people is interested in a Guinea cargo. "

The Gentleman's Magazine; April 1798

Introduction

Between 1699 and 1807 Liverpool grew from a small port into a large bustling town. There were a number of factors in this development and not least among these was the slave trade, also known as the "Guinea Trade" or the "West Africa Trade". The buying of human beings, transporting them from their homes in Africa before selling them as slaves in the Americas, was a heinous crime against humanity perpetuated by many European nations and with a ruthless efficiency by the merchants and sea captains of Liverpool. In around 5,000 voyages approximately 1.5 million men, women and children were carried in Liverpool ships from Africa to the Americas.

The abolition of the slave trade in 1807 was not, however, the end of Liverpool's involvement in slavery. Slave trading was profitable and it did not end in 1807. A ship that sailed from Liverpool in 1862 was apprehended by the Royal Navy off the coast of West Africa whilst attempting to engage in the slave trade. Liverpool people, at many levels, were compensated under the Slavery Abolition Act of 1833 when they were compelled to free enslaved people on plantations in the West Indies. Goods cultivated by enslaved people were imported into Liverpool in huge quantities from many places in the Americas – these were the very goods that had started the slave trade.

During the American Civil War some Liverpool merchants made fortunes speculating on cotton from the Southern States of America and actively supported Confederates in Liverpool as they built warships and blockade runners which lengthened the war and hence the enslavement of African Americans.

It was always inevitable that all of this involvement by Liverpool people would leave permanent marks on the city either physical or psychological. This book aims to explore street names in Liverpool and their links with slavery. In addition to the streets mentioned there are, of course, buildings which have connections with slavery including the Town Hall, the former Heywood's Bank in Brunswick Street and numerous properties which were the homes of people involved, in one way or another, in slavery.

With regard to the psychological scars still borne within the city, no book can begin to address these but in 2019 Liverpool elected its first black Lord Mayor and its first black Member of Parliament. Liverpool City Council voted early in 2020 to add interpretation boards to street signs with a link to slavery. In June 2020, as I was finishing writing this book, the toppling of the Colston statue in Bristol and demonstrations by the Black Lives Matter organisation started a conversation in the UK and around the world. I sincerely hope that this book will add to that conversation.

David Hearn BA(Hons) MA
June 2020

"Modern Liverpool, while being aware of this shameful History, appears to try hard to gloss over it, if not forget it.

- T Gifford, W Brown, and R Bundey
Loosen the Shackles – First report of the Liverpool 8 inquiry into race relations in Liverpool
(London: Karia Press, 1989)

ABERCROMBY SQUARE

Lieutenant General Ralph Abercromby (also spelt Abercrombie) was a British Army officer who was responsible for securing the West Indies island of Grenada after a pro-French revolt in 1794. He went on to capture the islands of Saint Lucia, Saint Vincent and Trinidad in the West Indies as well as taking possession of the territories of Demerara and Esquibo in what is now present day Guyana. Many Liverpool merchants and slave traders had cause to be thankful to General Abercromby for the wealth that his actions brought them.

Over the years a number of people with slavery connections have lived in Abercromby Square: 4 Abercromby Square was the home, at different times, of John Deane Case (1786-1859) and Henry Moore (1800-1852). John Deane Case was involved in 1 slave voyage in 1806 and was a member of Liverpool Council. In 1833, he was Treasurer of Liverpool. He received £3,720 by way of compensation under the Slavery Abolition Act of 1833 in respect of 182 enslaved people on an estate he owned in Saint Vincent. John Deane Case was a founder, with Sir Love Parry Price and Ambrose Lace,

of the North and South Wales Bank in 1810. The North and South Wales Bank merged with the Midland Bank in 1908. The Midland Bank became part of HSBC in 1999.

Henry Moore (1800-1852) was in partnership with his brother, Charles, in Moore Brothers who were West India merchants of Barbados and Liverpool. He was the recipient of just over £2,000 compensation under the Slavery Abolition Act of 1833 for 93 enslaved people who worked plantations he owned in Barbados and Tobago.

7 Abercromby Square was the home of Robertson Gladstone (1805-1875). Robertson was the son of John Gladstone - see Rodney Street - and older brother of William Ewart Gladstone who was four times Prime Minister of Great Britian. Along with his father, Robertson Gladstone was a West India merchant and sugar importer. He was also a partner in Heywood's Bank. Under the terms of the Slavery Abolition Act of 1833 Robertson Gladstone received compensation of over £21,000 in respect of enslaved people whom he was obliged to free

on an estate that he owned in British Guiana (now Guyana). Robertson Gladstone was Mayor of Liverpool 1842/43.

10 Abercromby Square was the home of Robert Preston who was a partner in the engineering company Fawcett Preston of York Street/Henry Street. Fawcett Preston were heavily involved in the design and manufacture of sugar refining equipment which was exported to the West Indies and, during the American Civil War, the company built the engines and guns of the Confederate commerce raider, CSS Alabama, as well as engines for several blockade runners.

Robert Preston sold 10 Abercromby Square to James Spence who was a supporter of slavery emancipation and had freed the enslaved people on a plantation he inherited from his father before he was obliged to. James Spence was, however, a strong supporter of the Confederate cause in the American Civil War, writing two best-selling books in support of the slave owning southern states. Spence was also instrumental in the arrangements to hold a Grand Southern Bazaar in St George's Hall to raise money for Southern prisoners of war. James Spence later contributed money to assist in the education of the sons of defeated Confederate President, Jefferson Davis, in both Canada and Liverpool.

11 Abercromby Square was the home of Robert Gladstone Jnr another son of John Gladstone - see Rodney Street. Robert received a half share of compensation of £9,225 when he was obliged to free 428 enslaved people on a plantation that he co-owned in Jamaica.

19 Abercromby Square was built by Charles Kuhn Proileau the Liverpool managing partner of the American cotton and banking firm Fraser Trenholm & Co. Although he was from Charleston, South Carolina, Proileau was a naturalised British citizen and had married a Liverpool woman, Mary Elizabeth Wright. Even before the American Civil War had started, Proileau had bought a state of the art rifled artillery piece from Fawcett Preston in Liverpool and sent it to his home city. When Fort Sumter in Charleston harbour was bombarded in April 1861, at the very start of the American Civil War, the gun supplied by Proileau was involved in the attack, giving rise to the often stated comment that the gun that fired the first shot in the war was made in Liverpool. The house retains many symbols of the Southern states of America and Proileau was a crucial political and financial supporter of the Confederacy during the American Civil War.

Left: Charles Kuhn Proileau house

20 Abercromby Square was, for a time, home to brothers Charles and Lewin Mozley who were partners in the Liverpool bank Israel Barned & Co. The brothers and the bank had strong connections with the southern states of America during the American Civil War and made loans to many Liverpool firms who bought cotton from the slave owning Southern states. Charles Mozley was Mayor of Liverpool 1863-64. An earlier member of the Mozley family, Morris Lewin Mozley, was involved in six slave voyages between 1799 and 1800.

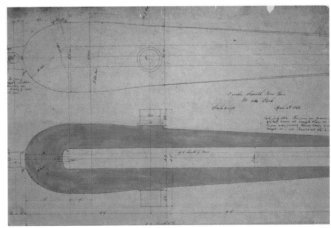

Above (Clockwise): Proileau family and Palmetto tree 19 Abergromby Sq; 1840 Head Office North and South Wales Bank, James St; Barned's Building, Sweeting Street. Alabama Pivot Gun – Fawcett Preston Plan

AIGBURTH HALL ROAD AND AIGBURTH HALL AVENUE

The original Aigburth Hall was a medieval building that passed into the hands of the Tarleton Family. The Tarleton family demolished the original structure and built a new hall but this too has now been demolished and there are no remains of either house. The Tarletons were originally from Fazakerley but later lived in a house that stood on the corner of Water Street and Fenwick Street. The building currently on the site carries a plaque marking it as birthplace of General Sir Banastre Tarleton (1754-1833) who was a soldier, then MP for Liverpool for many years - see Banastre Street. The Tarleton family were merchants and ship owners but, over three generations, they were also extensive slave traders. Between 1717 and 1802 various members of the Tarleton family were involved in 204 slave voyages. In some of these voyages several members of the family were part-owners of the same ship, sometimes a family member was the sole owner and in other voyages there were other partners. The number of individual investments by members of the Tarleton family in slave voyages was 316. Such was the depth of involvement in the slave trade that in two voyages the executors of Clayton Tarleton participated in voyages after his death. Jane Tarleton was one of a very small number of Liverpool women who were involved in slave voyages - she participated as a part-owner of a ship in three voyages between 1797 and 1799. John Tarleton V (1755-1841) was also a sugar baker and he was involved in whaling while Thomas Tarleton (1753-1820) was involved in the sugar business with John and was also partner in an insurance brokerage. Both John and Thomas were members of the Liverpool Chamber of Commerce. Thomas Tarleton owned a plantation in Grenada on which 256 enslaved people worked. This plantation had been left to him by his father John Tarleton IV (1718-1773). John Tarleton V also owned a plantation which was worked by 46 enslaved people on the island of St Lucia. John Tarleton IV was Mayor of Liverpool in 1764/65 and Clayton Tarleton was Mayor of Liverpool 1792/93. See also - Tarleton Street.

ASHFIELD

James Clemens built a house called Ashfield in Wavertree, which was then the leafy countryside surrounding Liverpool. Clemens was a captain, part-owner or owner of a number of ships in 38 slave voyages between 1753 and 1785. James Clemens became a member of the Common Council of Liverpool in 1767 and was Mayor 1775/6. During his time as Mayor he presented a 2 cwt (104kg) bell to St Paul's Church in Stoneycroft.

ALABAMA WAY,
BIRKENHEAD

By the time of the American Civil War the ties Liverpool had with America already went back almost 200 years. By 1860 the immense importance of cotton in Liverpool's trade meant that there were many well established business and personal connections with the slave owning southern or Confederate states. There was much intrigue in Liverpool in support of the Confederacy during the war which, undoubtedly, prolonged the war and delayed the emancipation of enslaved people in America. The chief foreign agent in Britain for the Confederacy during the American Civil War was James Dunwoody Bulloch (1823-1901) who was born in Georgia in the United States of America. The US State Department referred to Bulloch as "the most dangerous man in Europe". Bulloch arrived in Liverpool within two months of the start of the American Civil War and set up his headquarters in the offices of Fraser, Trenholm & Company in Rumford Place, Liverpool. Various plaques and signs have been attached to the Rumford Place building as if in some sort of 'celebration' of the involvement of Liverpool in the American Civil War. Bulloch had two roles in Liverpool. Firstly to organise ships to break the blockade that the US Federal government had imposed on the Southern ports which would enable cotton to be exported payment for which would enable the Confederacy to buy much needed military supplies. Bulloch was also charged with creating a navy for the Confederate states. It would be impossible for Bulloch to create a navy which could challenge the United States fleet so he set about buying and building fast, heavily armed ships to act as "commerce raiders" which could disrupt the trade of the Northern states. Perhaps the most famous ship constructed by Bulloch was the CSS Alabama which was built in great secrecy at Lairds in Birkenhead while the engines and guns were made at Fawcett Preston in Lydia Ann Street, Liverpool. In her two year career the CSS Alabama became the most successful commerce raider in history. The Alabama stopped and boarded nearly 450 vessels and captured or burned 65 Union merchant ships – more merchant ships than the most successful German U-Boat of either the First or Second World wars. During her exploits CSS Alabama captured over 2,000 prisoners although there was no loss of life among either the prisoners or the crew of the Alabama. The CSS Alabama was sunk off Cherbourg, France on 19th June, 1864 during an action with the USS Kearsarge.

At the end of the American Civil War James Dunwoody Bulloch and his half-brother Irvine, who had served on the CSS Alabama and CSS Shenandoah, were initially excluded from the general amnesty granted to officers of the Confederate armed forces. Although later granted an amnesty, the Bulloch brothers remained in Liverpool with James dying at his daughter's house at 76 Canning Street while Irvine died in Colwyn Bay, North Wales. The brothers are buried next to each other in Toxteth Cemetery, Liverpool.

*Top row: 76 Canning Street; front page of the contract to build the Alabama; No 4 Dock at Lairds – where the Alabama was built;
Middle Row – Left and Right - Rumford Place, offices of Fraser Trenholm & Co; Middle Charles Dunwoody Bulloch and Irvine Bulloch graves,
Toxteth Cemetery
Bottom row: American Civil War plaques, Rumford Place*

ASPINALL STREET

Between 1765 and 1807 several members of the Aspinall family were involved in 197 slave voyages sometimes with other members of their family and sometimes with others as part-owners of ships. John Bridge Aspinall (died 1830) was Mayor of Liverpool in 1804 and he alone was involved in 113 slave voyages. Another member of the family, James Aspinall (1729-1787), was Mayor of Liverpool in 1834/5. The Aspinall family established links with other people involved in slavery in Liverpool through marriage. Elizabeth Aspinall, daughter of John Bridge Aspinall, married Richard Addison of Bank Hall who owned an estate in Jamaica and received compensation of £3,600 when he was obliged to free his enslaved people. In 1798 James Aspinall's daughter, Sarah, married John (later Sir John) Tobin – see Tobin Street, Wallasey - who had been a partner with members of the Aspinall family in a number of slave trading voyages and owned enslaved Africans on a plantation in Jamaica. John Bridge Aspinall's son, James, was the joint incumbent of St Luke's Church, Liverpool - now known as the "bombed out church".

ATHERTON STREET,
NEW BRIGHTON

James Atherton, the "founder of New Brighton" was involved as part-owner of the slave ship Sarah in one slave voyage in 1797/8 when 412 kidnapped Africans were taken to Jamaica. Other members of Atherton's family were involved in a total of 23 other slave voyages.

BALTIMORE STREET

Baltimore (now in the state of Maryland, USA) was the main port from which tobacco from Maryland was exported to Liverpool by Liverpool merchants including Samuel Hunter who owned the land on which the street now stands. Whenever there was a regular cargo coming into Liverpool there was always a return cargo and, in 1770, the biggest return cargoes were British and Irish linen and salt. See also Hunter Street, Virginia Street and Maryland Street.

A VIEW OF THE KING'S TOBACCO WAREHOUSES,
SITUATE ON THE EAST SIDE OF THE KING'S DOCK.

Left: St Luke's Church, Bold Place
Bottom Right: James Atherton head stone, St George's Church, Everton

BANASTRE STREET

Named after General Banastre Tarleton (1754-1833) (later Sir Banastre Tarleton) who was a 'hero' of the American Revolutionary War (or a villain from the point of view of the Americans who called him 'Bloody Ban' or 'Butcher Ban'). Tarleton led a unit of Americans who were loyal to Britain and was wounded three times. Banastre Tarleton was part of the merchant and slave trading Tarleton family who, over three generations between 1717 and 1802 were involved in no fewer than 204 slave voyages as captain, part-owners or owners of many slave ships. He was MP for Liverpool from 1790 to 1806 and, again, from 1807 to 1812. Although there is no evidence that Banastre Tarleton was directly involved in any slave voyages he both spoke against and voted against the abolition of the slave trade in 1807. See also – Tarleton Street and Aigburth Hall Road.

BASNETT STREET

Christopher Basnett was the first minister of the Key Street Chapel which was licenced in 1707 as a meeting place of the 'Protestant Dissenters'. Basnett Street was laid out between 1770 and 1780 and it is, therefore, more likely that it was named after Nathaniel Basnett because Christopher had died in 1744. Nathaniel Basnett was involved as a co-owner in 3 slave voyages between 1753 and 1757.

BECKWITH STREET

John Beckwith was involved in 8 slave voyages between 1759 and 1771. Of these 8 voyages the numbers of kidnapped Africans transported is only recorded in 6 cases but the total for those 6 voyages is 978 people.

BENSON STREET

Several members of the Benson family were heavily involved in the slave trade. Between 1747 and 1765 William Benson Jr was involved in 18 slave voyages and John Benson (1684-1766) was involved in 8 slave voyages. John Benson's son, Moses Benson (1738-1806), was a highly successful West India merchant who started his career as a captain for Lancaster merchant Abraham Rawlinson and became his agent in Jamaica. He returned to Liverpool a very wealthy man in the 1770's and undertook 83 slave voyages between 1783 and 1805. He was also involved in the lucrative but extremely risky business of privateering. He bought a substantial house in Duke Street, Liverpool which, together with its garden, occupied the whole block between Cornwallis Street, Kent Street and St James's Street. In common with other Liverpool slave traders, Benson was a benefactor in the town and in 1802 he built and endowed St James's School for poor children. He was also a Captain in the volunteer unit raised by John Bolton for the defence of Liverpool - see Bolton Street. The will of Moses Benson provides for the four of his six children who survived him although it makes no mention of their mother, Judith Powell. Judith Powell was born in Jamaica and is described as a "free mustee" which suggests that she was mixed race. Although he never married Judith Powell, she did accompany him and the children when they returned to Liverpool. Unlike other Liverpool slave traders, Moses Benson did not buy a country house during his lifetime. However, following his death the trustees of his will made considerable purchases - in 1810 they bought the Lutwyche Estate in Shropshire (pictured below) for £25,450. In the same year they bought Easthope, followed by Presthope in 1815, Church Stretton in 1817, Broome in 1824, Pentre Hall, Alcaston and Meadowsin in 1824 and Hopebowdler in 1833. By the 1830s the land holdings of the Benson family were worth £155,358.

BOLD STREET

Jonas Bold was a slave trader and, as a sugar boiler, he was a dealer in goods grown by enslaved people. He was involved in four slave voyages between 1770 and 1799. He leased the land that is currently Bold Street, Bold Place and the site of St Luke's Church from the Corporation. James and Jonathan Brookes operated a ropery on the site. Between 1791 and 1795 Bold was a partner in a bank with Thomas Staniforth, Francis Ingram and Joseph Dalterra. Thomas Staniforth was involved in 77 slave voyages between 1757 and 1806 and Francis Ingram was involved in 109 slave voyages between 1761 and 1804. Jonas Bold was Mayor of Liverpool 1802/3. In the year that he was Mayor, Jonas Bold lived in Redcross Street.

BOLTON STREET

John Bolton (1756-1837) was born in Ulverston but, like many before and after him, was drawn to Liverpool as the port expanded. He became an apprentice to Messrs Rawlinson and Chorley who were West India merchants and was sent to Saint Vincent in the West Indies. Bolton returned to Liverpool in the 1780s, having made a personal fortune of around £100,000, in Saint Vincent, to set himself up in business on his own account. Between 1787 and 1807 John Bolton was heavily involved in the trans-Atlantic slave trade undertaking 70 slave voyages as part-owner or, predominately, sole-owner of a number of slave ships. In 1803 when it was thought that France might invade Britain, John Bolton raised, clothed, armed and equipped, at his own expense, a regiment of 600 men for the defence of Liverpool. Bolton was the Colonel of this regiment which was somewhat ironically known as "Bolton's Invincibles". His second in command was Lt Colonel Thomas Parkes; Joseph Greaves was a Major and the Captains were Thomas Rodie, William Forbes, James Penny and Moses Benson. All of these officers were substantial slave traders. The regiment was disbanded in 1806 when the local militia was established. For some years John Bolton was in partnership with Anthony Littledale and they were prolific traders in cotton from British Guiana (now Guyana). Under the terms of the 1833 Slavery Abolition Act Bolton received over £27,800 in compensation when he was forced to free 635 enslaved people who worked on his plantations in British Guiana and Saint Vincent. Bolton was a member of the Liverpool Chamber of Commerce. During the first decade of the 19th century Bolton purchased a substantial country house on the edge of Lake Windermere known as Storrs Hall.

IN THE VAULT BENEATH ARE DEPOSITED THE REMAINS OF JOHN BOLTON ESQUIRE OF LIVERPOOL LATE OF STORRS HALL IN THIS PARISH BORN AT ULVERSTON 22ND MARCH 1756 DIED AT LIVERPOOL 21ST FEBRUARY 1837

ALSO OF ELIZABETH HIS WIFE DAUGHTER OF HENRY LITTLEDALE ESQ. BORN AT WHITEHAVEN 19TH NOVEMBER 1768. DIED AT STORRS HALL 22ND OF SEPTEMBER 1848.

BOOKER AVENUE

Josias Booker (1793-1865) went to Demerara (now part of Guyana) in 1815 and became the attorney for the Broom Hall Estate from 1818 to 1827. When he returned to Liverpool in 1827 Booker formed Josias Booker & Co, a highly successful West India merchant business. He bought the Old Dispensary in Post Office Place, Church Street, Liverpool (picured right) and spent a considerable sum renovating it. He hosted the initial meetings of the sponsors of what would become the Royal Insurance Company and he bought 1,000 of the initial 100,000 £20 shares. He was the first chairman of the Royal Insurance Company. Booker was also a ship owner as well as being involved in the formation of the Royal Bank of Liverpool in 1836 of which he was a Director in 1837 and Chairman in 1847. He was a governor and trustee of the Blue Coat Hospital and one of the founders of the Manor Hall Asylum in London, becoming a Life Governor from 1843 until his death. Booker was also one of the founders of St Anne's Church in Aigburth, Liverpool along with John Moss, Charles Stewart Parker and John Abraham Tinne. Moss, Parker and Tinne were all recipients of considerable sums of money in compensation when enslaved people were emancipated under the Slavery Abolition Act of 1833.

Blackburne House heavily altered in the 1870s.

BLACKBURNE PLACE

Between 1748 and 1761 John Blackburn(e) Sr was involved in 11 slave voyages and John Blackburn(e) Jnr was involved in 4 slave voyages. John Blackburn was a producer of salt which was a valuable export commodity for Liverpool. Salt was shipped to Africa as a product for barter and was extensively used as a trade good in the West Indies and the North American colonies. John Blackburn Jr was Mayor of Liverpool 1760/61.

BLUNDELL LANE

Blundell Lane is a private pedestrian road which runs from School Lane to College Lane in Liverpool city centre between the Quaker Meeting House and the Bluecoat Chambers. It is named in honour of Bryan Blundell (1675-1756) in acknowledgement of his contribution to the establishment of the Bluecoat School. Bryan Blundell's contribution towards the cost of the Blue Coat School was £250 which, by present standards, seems modest. However, to put the donation into context, the cost of the school house was £35 and the annual salary of the school master was £20. Given that the Liverpool Society of Friends (Quakers) were at the forefront of the movement to abolish the slave trade, it seems unusual that their modern successors have chosen to honour Bryan Blundell who was personally involved in 3 slave voyages between 1721 and 1726. He was Mayor of Liverpool 1721/2 and again 1728/29. His son, Henry Blundell was Mayor of Liverpool 1793/94 and his grandson Henry Blundell-Hollinshead was Mayor 1807/08. Including Bryan Blundell, three generations of the Blundell family were involved both in slave trading and in the governance of the Blue Coat School. There was a continued philanthropic interest in the Blue Coat School from people who were involved in the slave trade in Liverpool. In 1741 there were 49 trustees of the Blue Coat School and, of these, 27 were directly involved in the slave trade. See also – Blundell Street.

BLUNDELL STREET

The Blundell family were involved in a total of 114 slave voyages and they were also dealers in goods from the West Indies which were cultivated by enslaved people. Jonathan Blundell (c.1723-1800) was a sugar baker with Black, Hodgson and Sparling and later became a canal proprietor with William Earle and Edward Chaffers – all people who were involved in the trans-Atlantic slave trade. Different generations of the Blundell family maintained their close connection with the Blue Coat School (pictured right) and served as trustees and governors over the years. See also – Blundell Lane.

BROOKS ALLEY

Brothers, John and Joseph Brooks were builders and ropemakers who lived in Hanover Street. An alley was subsequently laid through the garden of their house and was named after the family. Although John Brooks was, apparently, not involved in the slave trade, his brother Joseph and other members of the Brooks were major slave traders who participated in a total of 50 slave voyages between 1748 and 1791. Joseph Brooks' son, also called Joseph, was a turpentine manufacturer, a rope maker and a brewer. He is perhaps best known as the owner of the slave ship "Brooks" of which William Elford and the Plymouth Society for Effecting the Abolition of the Slave Trade produced the infamous illustration in late 1788. This showed how people kidnapped from Africa were packed into a ship with very little room for the notorious "Middle Passage" - the journey from Africa to the Americas. The image was originally produced on a broadsheet in Bristol before being republished by the London branch of the Society with copies sent to all MP's in 1789.

BROUGHAM TERRACE

Brougham Terrace was named in honour of Henry Peter Brougham, 1st Barron Brougham and Vaux (1778-1868) when it was originally built in the 1830s. Brougham played a major part in the 1833 Slavery Abolition Act. At this time Brougham was Lord High Chancellor of Great Britain. He stood in the 1812 General Election as one of the two Whig candidates in Liverpool but he was heavily defeated. Brougham Terrace was later expanded and was used as local government offices. After 1834 Brougham held no high office, although he was raised to the peerage in 1830. It became public knowledge in 1838 that in many British colonies emancipation of enslaved people was still being obstructed, former enslaved people were being discriminated against and badly treated Brougham spoke in the House of Lords, saying:
"The slave … is as fit for his freedom as any English peasant, aye, or any Lord whom I now address. I demand his rights; I demand his liberty without stint … I demand that your brother be no longer trampled upon as your slave!"
Numbers 8 to 10 Brougham Terrace became the Liverpool Muslim Institute which was founded in 1887 by William Henry Quilliam also known as Abdullah Quilliam. A small Mosque had been established in 8 Brougham Terrace by 1889 which is widely accepted as being the first Mosque in the United Kingdom. 8 Brougham Terrace is Listed Grade II*.

CAMPBELL STREET

Several members of the Campbell family were involved in the slave trade -
George Campbell (Sr) was involved in 41 slave voyages between 1735 and 1765;
George Campbell (Jr) was involved in 13 slave voyages between 1758 and 1766;
Mungo Campbell was involved in 20 slave voyages between 1733 and 1752.
The family were also sugar merchants. George Campbell (Sr) was Mayor of Liverpool
1763/64.

CARNATIC ROAD

A house was built on this site in 1779 by Peter Baker and John Dawson, the land
having been previously owned by the Ogden family. The house was called Carnatic
Hall after Baker's ship the Mentor which, under the command of John Dawson,
captured a French East Indiaman called "Carnatic". The ship was carrying a cargo
valued at around £135,000. Peter Baker was to become John Dawson's father-in-
law and was Mayor of Liverpool in 1795, although he died during his year in office.
Between 1768 and 1789 Peter Baker was involved in 49 slave voyages many of which
in partnership with his son-in-law John Dawson. Dawson was involved in a total of
126 slave voyages between 1760 and 1797.

CASES STREET

Four members of the Case family were responsible, between them, for 194 slave
voyages, transporting thousands of kidnapped Africans to lives of toil and misery
in the Americas. John Deane Case was involved in one slave voyage in 1806 and
Thomas Case Jnr was also involved in one slave voyage in 1807. Thomas Case Snr
was a part-owner of ships involved in 43 slave voyages between 1763 and 1776. In
common with others who were involved in the trans-Atlantic slave trade, Thomas
Case had other business interests. He was a West India merchant, had interests in a
colliery as well as being a coal agent with Gregson and Clayton. He was also involved
in glass manufacturing and real estate. Thomas Case was a member of the Liverpool
Chamber of Commerce. George Case was owner or part-owner of ships involved in
149 slave voyages in the 30 years between 1777 and 1807. To have the capital to equip
that number of voyages suggests that George Case was a very wealthy man. George
Case (1747-1836) was Mayor of Liverpool 1781/82.

CAZNEAU STREET

In the 1777 Liverpool street directory Joseph Cazneau is described as a 'merchant' living at 18 Hanover Street while his son, Benjamin, is a 'Captain' living at the same address. At this time Hanover Street was still a desirable address although it would not be long before people with money would start to move "up the hill" onto Mount Pleasant and, a little later, to Rodney Street and beyond to get away from the smoke and smells of the town centre. Even now Cazneau Street is still removed from the city centre and this is what would have attracted Joseph Cazneau to choose it as an area for him to have his retirement home built there in 1796. Joseph Cazneau engaged in 9 slave voyages between 1765 and 1787 while Benjamin Cazneau was involved in 3 slave voyages between 1777 and 1788.

CHORLEY STREET

John Chorley (c.1735-c.1810) was a merchant and ship-owner originally from Lancaster. He was in partnership with Abraham Rawlinson as West India merchants and tanners. John Chorley was involved in 5 slave voyages between 1752 and 1776. His business partner, Abraham Rawlinson was involved as part-owner of ships in 4 slave voyages between 1749 and 1776.

CLAYTON SQUARE

William Clayton was a slave trader, dealer in slave grown goods and MP for Liverpool from 1701 to 1708 and again from 1713 to his death in 1715. He imported tobacco from Virginia and Maryland, which were British colonies at the time, as well as sugar from Montserrat, Antigua and St Kitts, British colonies in the West Indies. Both the tobacco and sugar in all these areas would have been cultivated by enslaved people. William Clayton was in partnership with John Earle in the first three slave ships which left Liverpool - the "Liverpool Merchant" and the Unicorn of 1699 and the "Africa" of 1700. Of those first three ships, the number of kidnapped Africans carried is only recorded for the Liverpool Merchant, which carried 220 people to a life of toil, abuse and misery - the first of approximately 1.5 million men, women and children carried on Liverpool ships to the Americas between 1699 and 1807. In total, William Clayton was involved in 5 slave voyages between 1699 and 1710.

CLEVELAND SQUARE

John Cleveland (sometimes spelled Clieveland) was Mayor of Liverpool in 1703/04 and MP for Liverpool from 1710 to 1713. He was a sugar and tobacco merchant and was involved in 4 slave voyages between 1710 and 1716. The sugar and tobacco bought and sold by John Cleveland would, of course, have been cultivated by enslaved people. John's son, William Cleveland was also MP for Liverpool from 1722 to 1724.

CLARENCE STREET

Clarence Street was named after the Duke of Clarence who was given the Freedom of Liverpool in 1799 in recognition of him speaking in the House of Lords in favour of continuance of the slave trade. Whereas most streets named after people involved in slavery are named because an individual had a connection, either residential or business, with an area, this is an example of a person being honoured by the Common Council of Liverpool for no other reason than their support of the slave trade.

COLQUITT STREET

Scrope Colquitt was a part-owner of a number of ships involved in ten slave voyages between 1747 and 1755. There were a number of generations of the Colquitt family all of whom had the first name Scrope. One of the Scrope Colquitts married Frances (nee Milner) in 1792. Frances Colquitt was an "absentee slave-owner" in Jamaica. She effectively owned enslaved people as a form of investment and received compensation of over £1,159 in respect of 71 enslaved people on Jamaica when she was forced to free them. While £1,159 might not seem to be a great sum, a private in a British Army line regiment would be earning around £19 a year at the time equivalent to 61 years' salary.

COMBERMERE STREET

Combermere Street was named in honour of Lieutenant General Stapleton Cotton, 1st Viscount Combermere, who received the Freedom of Liverpool in 1821. Viscount Combermere was awarded compensation of £5,334 under the 1833 Slavery Abolition Act in respect of enslaved people he owned in Nevis and St Kitts.

COOK STREET

Charles Cook (Cooke) was a merchant who was involved in 39 slave voyages as part-owner of ships between 1749 and 1771.

COTTON STREET

Liverpool was the principle UK port involved in the importation of cotton much of it from countries where the crops were cultivated by enslaved people. Although cotton had come into Britain earlier, the first recorded importation of cotton into Liverpool was in 1757 when 28 bags of Jamaican cotton were offered for sale in a Liverpool newspaper. By 1770, only 13 years later, 6,027 bags of cotton were imported from the West Indies and very small amounts were arriving from North and South Carolina, Virginia and Georgia in the American colonies. In the same year Joshua Holt became Liverpool's first cotton broker. In 1795 Liverpool became the country's leading cotton importation port over London. By 1829 there were 45 cotton broking firms in Liverpool, 111 by 1841, 161 in 1851 and by 1860 there were 322. Until the emancipation of the enslaved people in the United States the majority of cotton imported through Liverpool was grown by enslaved people.

CROPPER STREET

Cropper Street may have been named after James Cropper or Edward Cropper. James Cropper was a merchant and ship owner as well as a supporter of the campaign to abolish the slave trade as were many of his fellow Liverpool members of the Quaker faith. Edward Cropper, on the other hand, was involved as a captain or part-owner of a number of slave ships between 1750 and 1767 which were involved in a total of 40 slave voyages.

CROSBIE STREET

Between 1745 and 1780 four members of the Crosbie family, James, John, William Sr and William Jr were involved in a total of 189 slave voyages. James Crosbie was Mayor of Liverpool 1753/4. John Crosbie was Mayor of Liverpool 1765/6. William Crosbie was mayor of Liverpool 1776/77. William Crosbie Jr was Mayor of Liverpool 1779/80. The Crosbie family were also involved in privateering whereby privately owned armed ships were given permission to attack and capture the merchant ships of countries with whom Britain was at war.

CROW STREET

Crow Street in Liverpool 8 named after Captain Hugh Crow (1765-1829). The 1807 street directory shows him as living in King Street although it also lists there being a King Street in Edge Hill, Pool Lane and Soho/St Anne's Street. Although he ended his life in Preston, it is possible that Crow retired and moved out of Liverpool town centre for a while. Whether it was named for Hugh Crow or not, he is worthy of mention for two reasons. Firstly, that he is one of a few, if not the only, captains to write his memoirs and, secondly, because he was the captain of one of the last legal slave voyages to leave Liverpool.

Crow was from the Isle of Man and lost an eye as a child. His first voyage was from Whitehaven to the West Indies in 1782 when he would have been 22/23. He also sailed to the Baltic several times and to the United States of America before becoming Chief Mate on a slave voyage in 1790 and, in 1798, becoming the captain of a slave ship for his first of seven voyages in that role.

In his memoirs Crow, portrays himself as fierce fighter against any French ships and as a kindly and generous captain to the kidnapped Africans on his ships. His consideration does, perhaps, have a basis in truth because following the 1788 'Dolben's Act', captains were paid a bounty if the mortality rate was 3% or under and double the amount if the mortality rate was 2% or under. In his last slave voyage as Captain of the Kitty's Amelia, Crow claimed a bounty of £828 16s [£828.80] in respect of 280 Africans. Considering that the pay for a Captain might have been six guineas [£6 6s/£6.30] per month this would have been a considerable sum.

While Crow may have been compassionate he never apparently questioned the morality of the trade in which he was involved and, like others involved in the slave trade, he believed that Africans might have had better lives in the Americas than they had in their home countries.

Captain Hugh Crow (1765-1829)

" ... factory children in England grew up 'in a state of almost as great ignorance and deadness of heart as the negroes of the West Indies' and that the material conditions of the Irish and some of the English poor were worse than those of slaves.

- William Gladstone
Address to the electors of Newark, 6 December 1832

CUNLIFFE STREET

Between 1718 and 1760 three members of the Cunliffe family - Ellis, Foster and Robert were involved in a total of 67 slave voyages. Foster Cunliffe was described as Liverpool's leading merchant and one source at least suggests that he was the biggest businessman in the whole country although with the pre-eminence of London this seems an unlikely accolade. In the mid-18th century Ellis and Robert Cunliffe were owners or part-owners of 26 ships. Of these at least four were regular slaving ships with a combined capacity to carry 1,120 kidnapped Africans. In common with other Liverpool slave traders the Cunliffe family made alliances through marriage, Foster Cunliffe's elder sister married Charles Pole, a slave trader and West India merchant who was chairman of Sun Fire Insurance and MP for Liverpool from 1756 to 1761. Foster Cunliffe's younger sister married Bryan Blundell who was also a slave trader and West India merchant. Ellis (later Sir Ellis) Cunliffe was MP for Liverpool from 1755 to 1767. Foster Cunliffe was Mayor of Liverpool 1716/17, 1729/30 and 1735/36. Robert Cunliffe was Mayor of Liverpool 1758/59.

DEANE STREET

The Deane family were heavily involved in a number of different aspects of the slave trade. Edward Deane (Sr) was involved in 15 slave voyages between 1744 and 1761 while Edward (Jr) was involved in 3 slave voyages between 1787 and 1788. Richard Deane was a partner in the large Liverpool West India merchant firm of Barton, Ireland & Higginson and received over £31,400 in compensation for freeing 1,433 enslaved people in Barbados following the Slavery Abolition Act of 1833.

DORANS LANE

When both father and son had the same name as is the case with Felix Doran it is not always easy to differentiate between the activities of the two generations. Felix Sr died in 1776 although this does not mean that his son was not involved in slave trading before that date. Between 1737 and 1793 father and son were involved as part-owners of various slave ships in 99 slave voyages. Groups of investors often, although not always, maintained a business relationship for a number of years. Felix Doran Jr married Thomas Foxcroft's niece, Mary. Thomas Foxcroft had undertaken a number of slave voyages with Felix Doran Sr and this continued after Felix Sr died. Felix Jr was involved in a number of voyages with Thomas Foxcroft as well as Foxcroft's nephew George Welch and another relative, James Welch.

DENISON STREET

Like a number of other slave traders William Denison initially operated his business from Lancaster but, during the 1760s, he moved his operation to Liverpool. William Denison, father and son, were, between them, involved in 32 slave voyages between 1763 and 1794.

EARLE ROAD/EARLE STREET

In common with other Liverpool families the Earle family were major slave traders over three generations. John Earle was part owner with William Clayton - see also Clayton Square - of the first two slave ships which left Liverpool. Members of the Earle family were involved in at least 270 slave voyages carrying a total of around 40,000 kidnapped Africans to the Americas. The family involvement in slavery stretches from 1699 to 1804. William Earle Snr (1721-1788) had various other business interests. He operated a packet service to Leghorn (Livorno, Italy) as well as being a major ship owner with Thomas Hodgson, Ingram and Leyland all of whom were major investors in the trans-Atlantic slave trade. In addition, he was an ironmonger and anchor smith. William Earle Snr was a member of the Liverpool Chamber of Commerce. Many wealthy Liverpool families had country houses as well as their town house and the Earle family was no exception. Their country house was Allerton Towers. Three different members of the family became Mayors of Liverpool; John Earle was Mayor 1709/10; Ralph Earle was Mayor 1769/70 and William Earle Jr was Mayor 1836/37.

Left; All that remains of Allerton Towers; Right: Earle Street

EWART STREET

William Ewart (????-1823), was a West India merchant who made considerable profits from crops cultivated by enslaved people. William Ewart also owned a share in a cotton mill and was a mortgagee of a plantation in Demerara. William Ewart was a partner in the firm Ewart and Rutson who were general and cotton merchants in Liverpool. William's son, also called William, was MP for Liverpool from 1830 to 1837. John Gladstone – see also Rodney Street - named his fourth son after William Ewart. William Gladstone would go on to be Prime Minister of Great Britain four times.

FAIRFIELD STREET

Fairfield Street is the site of the house known as Fairfield Hall which was built by Thomas Tarleton. The Tarleton family – see also Tarleton Street - were merchants and large scale slave traders. Between 1773 and 1799 Thomas Tarleton was involved in 85 slave voyages. Fairfield Hall was later owned by Edward Falkner - see Falkner Square/Falkner Street.

For further particulars apply to Mr. Statham or Mr. Leigh, attornies, in Liverpool.

BANKRUPT's EFFECTS.
TO BE SOLD BY AUCTION,
In the Great Room, at the Golden Lion, in Dale-street, *To-morrow*, the 28th inst. at eleven o'clock in the forenoon,

131 Bags Pernambucco COTTON,
73 Ditto Demerara Ditto,
138 Ditto St. Domingo Ditto,
404 Ditto Barbadoes Ditto,
663 Ditto common West India Ditto,
95 Ditto Carthagena Ditto.

Which may be seen in the mean time, and catalogues had by applying to   EWART and RUTSON, Brokers.

By Order of the Assignees of JOHN WATTS, a Bankrupt.
To be Peremptorily SOLD by AUCTION

Gore's Liverpool General Advertiser – Thursday June 27th, 1793

FALKNER SQUARE

Edward (later Sir Edward) Falkner was High Sheriff of Lancashire in 1788. By 1807, according to the Liverpool street directory for that year, Edward Falkner was living at Fairfield and was the 'Receiver General of the Land Tax etc for the County of Lancaster' with an office in Fleet Street, Liverpool. Edward Falkner bought some land which was known as Moss Lake Fields with a view to developing it as an upmarket residential area. There was initial reluctance from prospective buyers because it was at the top of a considerable hill and too far out of town. The development did go ahead with a square of fine villas surrounding a park. Edward Falkner lived at Fairfield in Liverpool. The park area in the centre of the square includes an interpretation board which refers to Edward Falkner as a "soldier" for no other reason than in 1797 he commanded the volunteers raised to defend Liverpool from a threatened French invasion in 1797. However, the board

FALKNER STREET

fails to mention that Edward Falkner was involved in 20 slave voyages between 1780 and 1807. While the board, which in June 2020 is in a rather sorry state, does not mention Falkner's slavery past, it does mention that "close by" is the site of Liverpool's first Botanic Garden "founded by William Roscoe". There is, perhaps, a certain irony that what the Liverpool Echo referred to in 2019 as the "forgotten Liverpool war memorial", a memorial to Black Merchant Seamen of the Second World War is located in Falkner Square. The memorial does now appear on local road signs but is still not situated with the other Merchant and Royal Navy memorials at Liverpool Pier Head. See also – Lee Hall Park for mention of an interpretation board which fails to mention slave trade history while mentioning an abolitionist not connected with the area.

FAZAKERLEY STREET

John Fazakerley (also spelt Fazackerly) was either a captain or part owner of a slave ship in 6 voyages between 1748 and 1774. In 1780 John paid £12 to have the Freedom of Liverpool.

FINCH LANE

Finch Lane gets its name from Finch House built by Richard Gildart in 1776. Richard Gildart was the son-in-law and business partner of Sir Thomas Johnson – see Sir Thomas Street.. He was a sugar and tobacco merchant and undertook five slave voyages between 1714 and 1718. Richard Gildart was MP for Liverpool from 1734 to 1754 and was three times Mayor of Liverpool in 1714/15, 1731/32 and 1750/51.

FORBES STREET

Edward Forbes was either a captain or part owner of slave ships involved in 11 voyages between 1735 and 1753. Edward Forbes started his involvement in the trans-Atlantic slave trade as a captain of a ship owned by John Sparling – see also Sparling Street.

GILDART STEET

Richard Gildart was involved in 5 slave voyages between 1714 and 1718 and he and other members of his family were involved in a total of 72 slave voyages. Richard Gildart was the son-in-law of Sir Thomas Johnson – see Sir Thomas Street. Both Gildart and Johnson were heavily in debt to the Crown in respect of unpaid duty on tobacco that they had imported into Liverpool. Tobacco was an important barter commodity in West Africa when

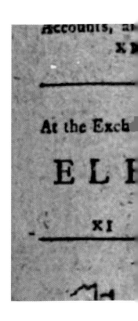

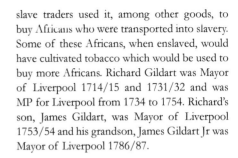

slave traders used it, among other goods, to buy Africans who were transported into slavery. Some of these Africans, when enslaved, would have cultivated tobacco which would be used to buy more Africans. Richard Gildart was Mayor of Liverpool 1714/15 and 1731/32 and was MP for Liverpool from 1734 to 1754. Richard's son, James Gildart, was Mayor of Liverpool 1753/54 and his grandson, James Gildart Jr was Mayor of Liverpool 1786/87.

GLADSTONE ROAD/STREET

These two streets were probably named after William Ewart Gladstone, the Liverpool born MP, who was four times Prime Minister. The entire Gladstone family were heavily involved in the slave trade. William Ewart's father, John, was involved in one slave voyage and was an extensive trader in goods cultivated by enslaved people – see Rodney Street. Under the Slavery Abolition Act of 1833 John Gladstone received £112,716 in compensation for freeing the enslaved people who worked on plantations which he owned in the West Indies. Robertson Gladstone, John Gladstone's son received compensation in respect of enslaved people in British Guiana (now Guyana) and was Mayor of Liverpool 1842/43. William Ewart Gladstone opposed the slave trade which would reduce the value of the enslaved people owned by his father but opposed the abolition of slavery until enslaved people had developed "honest and industrious habits" and there was better provision for their Christian education. In June 2020 the University of Liverpool took the decision to change the name of one of it's halls of residence from Gladstone Hall to an, as yet, undecided alternative.

GOREE

The section of The Strand named Goree is named after the Goree warehouses that stood on the site from 1793 until they were eventually demolished in 1958. The warehouses were almost completely destroyed by fire in 1802 but were rebuilt in 1811. The warehouses took their name from Ile de Goree (Goree Island) an island off the coast of Dakar in Senegal which was a notorious site in the trans-Atlantic slave trade. There is a persistent and false urban myth that set within the walls of these warehouses are hoops to which slaves were chained. Whilst some black people were undoubtedly brought to Liverpool, and indeed sold here, there were not many.

GRAYSON STREET

Between 1743 and 1749 John Grayson was involved as captain or part owner of various slave ships in 6 slave voyages. Anthony Grayson (1719-1785) was a timber merchant and a ship builder with Foster Cunliffe. He was a member of the Liverpool Chamber of Commerce and was involved in 28 slave voyages between 1744 and 1766. Edward Grayson was involved in 20 slave voyages between 1765 and 1800. Grayson was killed in a duel fought in Liverpool in 1804.

GREGSON STREET

The Gregson family was well established in Liverpool as merchants but with the growth of the slave trade the family saw its wealth and social position increase greatly. Between 1744 and 1800 William and John Gregson were involved in a total of 197 slave voyages carrying over 58,000 Africans to slavery in the Americas. William Gregson was Mayor of Liverpool 1762/63. John Gregson (1755-1802) was Mayor of Liverpool 1784/85 and he was also receiver of taxes for Lancashire. Three members of the Gregson family – William, John and James were part owners along with Edward Wilson and James Aspinall of the slave ship "Zong" which was involved in one of the most notorious recorded cases of abuse in the history of the trans-Atlantic slave trade. On 29th November 1781 and the days following more than 130 kidnapped Africans were murdered by being thrown overboard from the ship as it neared the port of Black River in Jamaica. When the Zong arrived in Jamaica the ship's owners claimed on their insurance policy for the loss of some of the "cargo" but the insurers refused the claim. The Gregson syndicate sued the insurers (Gregson v Gilbert (1783) 3 Doug. KB 232) and it was held that the deliberate killing of slaves was legal and the insurers would be required to pay the value of the people killed. The insurers who were led by Thomas Gilbert of Liverpool, who himself was involved in 5 slave voyages between 1770 and 1793, appealed the decision and the appeal court judges, chaired by the Earl of Mansfield who was Lord Chief Justice at the time, found against the Gregsons and their syndicate because new evidence suggested that the captain and crew were at fault. It is interesting that the appeal was not on the grounds that the crew had murdered anyone but rather that it was an attempted insurance fraud. The freed enslaved person, Olaudah Equiano and the abolitionist Granville Sharp campaigned to bring murder prosecutions against the captain and crew of the ship but without success. There is a memorial to those murdered on the Zong at Black River, Jamaica.

GRENVILLE STREET SOUTH

This street was named in honour of Lord Grenville (1759-1834) who succeeded William Pitt the Younger as Prime Minister from 11th February 1806 to 25th March 1807. In 1807 Grenville introduced the bill that abolished the slave trade and the Slave Trade Act, 1807 received it's royal assent on the last day of Grenville's Premiership. The street had originally been called Leveson Street but the name was changed in 1849 following a gruesome multiple murder. While it was undoubtedly of great importance in Britain and ultimately throughout Europe and North America, the abolition of the slave trade is all that the Grenville government achieved, having failed to secure either peace with France or Catholic emancipation which were the administration's other aims. The renaming of Leveson Street as Grenville Street could be seen, perhaps, as the start of a form of acceptance in Liverpool that the abolition of the slave trade was a positive step.

GREAT NEWTON STREET

Named after John Newton (1725-1807). John Newton was a captain on three slave voyages who, later in life, was ordained into the Church of England and wrote two famous hymns - Amazing Grace and Glorious Things of Thee are Spoken. John Newton sailed on four slave voyages from Liverpool. His first voyage was as First Mate on the ship "Brownlow" in 1748. Newton followed this with three voyages as a captain, on ships part-owned by his friend Joseph Manesty. The first voyage was on the ship "Duke of Argyle" between 1750 and 1751 which carried 146 kidnapped Africans from the Windward Coast to the island of Antigua. This voyage was followed by two voyages as skipper of the African 1752/53 and 1753/54 which both delivered kidnapped Africans to St Kitts - 167 and 87 people respectively. Before he was able to embark on another voyage Newton had a convulsive fit and was not able to resume work as a captain but Joseph Manesty secured him a job as a 'tide waiter' in Liverpool. Even though he was no longer able to captain a slave voyage he invested in a further voyage organised by Joseph Manesty. After his third voyage, during which there were no accidents and the ship did not lose a single man of either the crew or the kidnapped Africans, something which Newton believed was "The only instance of its kind" he wrote, "During the time I was engaged in the slave trade , I never had the least scruple as to its lawfulness. I was, upon the whole, satisfied with it ... It is indeed accounted a genteel employment, and is usually very profitable." Newton was ordained into the Anglican Church in 1764 but it was not until 1788, over 30 years after his last voyage, that he wrote a pamphlet called "Thoughts upon the African Trade" in which he apologises for his involvement in the slave trade. Newton sent copies of his pamphlet to every MP and became an ardent abolitionist. Although John Newton died in 1807 he lived long enough to see the abolition of the slave trade. There is a plaque to mark John Newton's residence in Edmund Street and a memorial to him was installed in the Mersey Ferry office at Liverpool's Pier Head in 2009 (pictured below). As of Summer 2020, the memorial is still in place. See also - Manesty's Lane.

"One of the best-known features of eighteenth-century British commercial history is the prominence of Liverpool as a slave-trading port."

- K. Morgan
Liverpool's Dominance in the British Slave Trade, 1740-1807', D. Richardson, S. Schwarz, & A. Tibbles, (eds), Liverpool and Transatlantic Slavery; Liverpool University Press; 2007

HARDMAN STREET

John Hardman (c.1694-1755) was a West India merchant in partnership with his brother James. A slave trader and MP for Liverpool from 1754 to 1755, he was involved in 35 slave voyages between 1728 and 1734. His son, also John, was involved in 41 slave voyages between 1730 and 1761. Business must have been good for John and James Hardman because in 1736 they were able to buy Allerton Hall (pictured below) for £7,700 and then pay to have extensive building works carried out to the property. Upon John's death Allerton Hall passed to his widow and was ultimately purchased by Liverpool attorney and abolitionist William Roscoe see – Roscoe Street - in 1779.

HIGHFIELD ROAD

Highfield Road takes its name from Highfield House (pictured below) which was built in 1763 by Thomas Wakefield who was a sugar baker and a part-owner in a 1758 slave voyage. There appears to be a connection between Thomas Wakefield and the Kendal banker John Wakefield because both men were involved in the production of 'Kendall cotton', a coarse woollen fabric popular in both West Africa and the West Indies. They were co-owners of the Gatebeck gunpowder mill at Sedgewick in Cumbria. James Hayes, a Liverpool slave trader, was also a partner in this business. Gunpowder or "African powder" was an important trade good in demand by slave traders who used it as a barter commodity in West Africa. Highfield House was later owned by Charlotte the Dowager Duchess of Athol and her son John, from whom Thomas Littledale, the Liverpool cotton merchant, bought it. The house became the headquarters of a religious sect before it was demolished in 1915.

HIGHFIELD HOUSE,
Lancashire, the Seat of
Thomas Littledale, Esq.

HOUGHTON STREET

Richard Houghton Jnr was involved in 7 slave voyages between 1754 and 1762. Houghton was a merchant with many overseas connections including the then North American colonies and the West Indies as well as Northern Europe and Ireland.

A VIEW OF THE QUAKERS' MEETING-HOUSE, HUNTER-STREET.

HUNTER STREET

Samuel Hunter was a tobacco trader who lived in Mount Pleasant. As a tobacco merchant he was trading in goods cultivated by enslaved people. He also laid out Maryland Street and Baltimore Street. See also Maryland Street and Baltimore Street. Samuel Hunter was involved as a part-owner of a slave ship in one slave voyage in 1756.

IRLAM ROAD, BOOTLE

This road is built on the site of Bootle Hall the home of George Irlam and his family. George was a partner in the firm Barton, Irlam & Higginson who were West India merchants dealing principally with Barbados. In the 1824 Liverpool Street directory the firm's address is given as Henry Street, Liverpool. George Irlam owned a share of a plantation on Barbados and received compensation of £2,726 under the Slavery Abolition Act, 1833 when he was obliged to free the 122 enslaved people who worked on this plantation.

JAMAICA STREET

Jamaica was the destination for over 1,300 slave voyages which started in Liverpool. Between 1741 and 1810 Liverpool slave ships delivered 391,914 kidnapped Africans to Jamaica to be sold into slavery. A number of Liverpool citizens owned plantations with enslaved people in Jamaica. The island was also the source for many and various goods which were imported into Liverpool including sugar, rum, cotton and mahogany. There was also a considerable trade in goods including, in 1770, such basic goods as beans, potatoes, considerable amounts of linen and cotton cloth and 77,780 pieces of earthenware. The European tastes were amply catered for with 22,979 bushels of salt and 5,500 gallons of malt spirits. Perhaps most chilling of the many items exported from Liverpool to Jamaica in that year was ' Whips ... 31 doz. and a half ".

JAMES STREET

William James (1734-1798) was involved in no fewer than 132 slave voyages between 1758 and 1776. Little is written about him except that at one stage he had 29 ships engaged in the slave trade. He also owned a number of plantations in Jamaica which produced sugar and rum and he was clearly a person of some considerable capital. He was able to finance many slave voyages without involving partners and others with just one other investor. In 1775, when he lived at Rainford Garden along with many other merchants involved in the slave trade, there was a series of riots over a number of days. The riots were the result of an attempt to reduce the wages of sailors from 30 shillings (£1.50) per month to 20 shillings (£1) per month. The family had retreated to their country home, Finch House, West Derby. The town house, and all its possessions, in Rainford Garden was destroyed. It is said that when the rioters ransacked the house they found a "little negro boy" hiding out of fear in a clock case. His fate is not recorded.

James died at his house in Clayton Square.

KNIGHT STREET

John Knight was involved in 119 slave voyages between 1744 and 1776 as either captain, part owner or owner of various slave ships. Knight was a merchant who had premises in Water Street and sold oak planks and pitch amongst other things. He was a Liverpool Alderman.

LAWRENCE ROAD

Charles Lawrence (1776-1853) was Mayor of Liverpool 1823/4, a West India merchant and the owner of a plantation in Jamaica which was worked by enslaved people and yet he is chiefly remembered as the first chairman of the Liverpool and Manchester Railway. Charles Lawrence's son, George Hall Lawrence, was also a West India merchant who was in business with his father at premises in Bridgewater Street. He received compensation following the release of enslaved people who worked on the plantation which his father had owned. He was Mayor of Liverpool 1846/47. Another of Charles Lawrence's sons was Edward Lawrence who was Mayor of Liverpool 1864/65. During the American Civil War Edward Lawrence was involved in 'blockade running' where ships carried goods in and out of southern ports through the blockade imposed by the American federal government. This assisted the Confederate cause by supplying war material and providing valuable cash, thus extending the duration of the war.

Drawn by S. Austin   Engraved by W. Le Petit.

WAVERTREE HALL,
THE SEAT OF CHARLES LAWRENCE, ESQ.

LEE HALL PARK

Lee Hall Park takes its name from Lee Hall which was built in 1773 by John Okill (c.1687-1773) who was a major ship builder and merchant. Between 1739 and 1758 Okill built 9 ships for the Royal Navy. In 1750 John Okill is shown as being a member of the Company of Merchants Dealing with Africa. However, various sources state that his interest in Africa was restricted to the import of timber and "teeth" (ivory) although this would seem not to be the case as he undertook 12 slave voyages as part-owner between 1747 and 1757. Lee Hall was not complete at the time of John Okill's death and it was left to his nephew, James, to complete the works. John Okill gave the lease for the land on which St Thomas's Church was built. St Thomas's Church, Park Lane has long since been demolished but there is a small park area on the site with an interpretation board which mentions John Okill as a 'timber merchant', William Pownall as a 'successful merchant, magistrate and ship builder' and Richard Tate as a 'wealthy and successful snuff and tobacco merchant'. The board fails to mention the 12 slave voyages undertaken by Okill, the 43 by Pownall and the 11 by Tate but it does go into some length about James Currie the 'noted abolitionist' who was not actually buried at the site. See also Faulkner Square for an interpretation board which mentions an abolitionist but not the more obvious slave trade history of others.

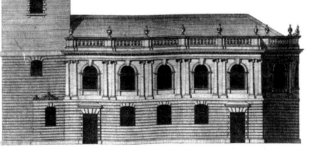

p.p. Burdett delin.

Edwd Rooker sculp.

St. Thomas's Church.

St Thomas' Memorial Garden

This garden has been placed on a corner of the former churchyard of St Thomas' Church, which was consecrated in 1750 and was the third church to be built in Liverpool. The land was donated by John Okill, a local timber merchant.

The church was designed by Henry Sephton and built at a cost of £5000. When construction was completed, the elegant church spire stood to a height that made it the tallest in the city. The graveyard was originally much larger but alterations to Paradise Street in 1885 meant that part of the graveyard was closed.

Two hundred years ago this area adjacent to the Old Dock and the developing Port was known as "Sailor Town" or the "Good Ole Town", a lively place where world-wide trade brought in exotic luxuries along with the cotton, sugar, wheat and tobacco on which Liverpool made its fortune.

Burials took place until the late 1800s', and many notable Liverpool citizens who contributed greatly to the development of the city were interred here: ship owners, merchants and sea captains, mayors and clergy, doctors and scientists and widows and children too.

The early twentieth century saw the population of the parish dwindle and this led to the church being closed. The last service was held on the 31st of December 1905.

Some of the stories of the people buried within this hallowed gro

Joseph Williamson

Joseph Williamson was buried in through his marriage to Richard 1802. Williamson successfully ma after Richard's death. An astute extraordinary tunnels at Edge Hi today. He died in 1840 aged 71 ye

Edmund

Edmund Richardson was a victim of the shipwreck of the which was wrecked at Formby Point, with 22 pilots, me drowned on the 29th of November 1883. Edm

Plot 24 & 25

William Pownall

William Pownall was born in 1719, and li He was a successful merchant, magistrate but died in office in 1768. Pownall Street a

William Hutchinson

Plot 239

William Hutchinson was born in 1715 in Newcastle-upon-Tyne, but it was in his adopted city of Liverpool that he flourished, making significant contributions to the success of the maritime city. He was multi-talented, assuming the roles of sea captain, Dock Master, inventor, author, politician, scientist and philanthropist during his lifetime. His Tide Tables are still internationally significant today. He died in 1801 aged 85 years.

Revd R.H Roughsedge

Plot 306

The Revd Robert Hankinson Roughsedge was born in Pool Lane, Liverpool in 1746. He was Chaplain of St Thomas' Church (1781-1794), minister at St George's (1794-96), and then Rector of Liverpool for 33 years until his death. He was greatly esteemed by the parishioners and died "old and full of days" in 1829 aged 83 years.

James Currie

Plot 153

The family of James Currie M.D. is buried here, along with his children Sarah and James. Currie was a noted abolitionist and a supporter of rights for the American and French prisoners of war. He championed hydrotherapy as a cure for fevers, publishing an extensive medical treatise at least 90 years before this was officially recognised as a treatment. Most famous as the biographer of the Scottish poet Robert Burns, he was also President of the Liverpool Athenaeum between 1801-1802. Currie died on a trip to the south and was buried there.

Richard Tate

Plot 221

Richard Tate was a successful and wealthy tobacco and snuff merchant. He was also a noted patron of the arts and helped to promote art in Liverpool. He was a keen painter and displayed his work at exhibitions in the city, one of which was the first art exhibition held in provincial England (outside of London) in 1774. He died in 1787, aged 51 years.

Margaret Swarbrick & Twentyman Family

Plot 21   Plot 294

'Here lie the remains of Margaret Swarbrick, she died April the fifteenth 1807 Aged 78 years.' The much loved and highly valued servant of Mrs Twentyman for forty eight years. The Twentyman's are also buried in St Thomas's. Their wealth is reflected in the fact that they could afford to purchase a significant plot for a family servant.

Andrew Fuhrer & Benedict Paul Wagner

Plot 253   Plot 281

Andrew Fuhrer and his business partner Benedict Paul Wagner, had premises on Mersey Street and are listed as Fuhrer and Wagner Merchants in the 1766 Gores Directory. As German immigrants, it is likely their families arrived in Britain as refugees from Southern Germany c.1709. Refugees fled the Palatinate states at this time due to political and religious upheaval. Many were shipped to New York from London. Several families settled in Liverpool, assimilated and set up successful businesses.

" ... while the people of Liverpool, in their indiscriminate rage for commerce and for getting money at all events, have nearly engrossed the Trade.

- W Matthews

The New History, Survey and Description of the City and Suburb of Bristol or Complete Guide and Bristol Directory for the year 1793-4; (Bristol, 1794) "

Drawn by G. & C. Pyne.

Engraved by R. Acon.

WATER STREET.

FISHER, SON & Cº LONDON, 1832.

LEIGH STREET

Between 1741 and 1767 Peers and James Leigh were involved in 25 slave voyages. Hugh Hindley Leigh (1738-1779), who was a member of Liverpool Chamber of Commerce and described in the Liverpool street directory as a 'Merchant' of 20 Water Street (pictured), was involved in 3 slave voyages between 1771 and 1776. Roger Leigh was involved as part-owner or owner of ships engaged in 12 slave voyages between 1795 and 1803. Other members of the Leigh family were also involved in the slave trade.

LORD NELSON STREET

In 1798 Lord Nelson was given the Freedom of Liverpool in acknowledgment not only of his abilities as an admiral but also because of his support of slavery and the slave trade. In his letter thanking Liverpool for the honour he wrote - 'I was taught to appreciate the value of our West India possessions, and neither in the field, nor in the senate, shall their interests be infringed while I have an arm to fight in their defence.'

MADDOCK ROAD, WALLASEY

John Maddock (sometimes spelt Maddocks) was a coal dealer with premises in Pemberton Alley. He was also involved in 24 slave voyages between 1745 and 1771 before buying Liscard Manor in Wallasey which, at the time, was a rural retreat and, doubtless, considered an agreeable place to retire to.

MANESTY'S LANE

Joseph Manesty was a part-owner and, in one case, the owner of various ships involved in 22 slave voyages between 1744 and 1758. This is an interesting situation, although Joseph Manesty was involved in the slave trade, his brother John was opposed to it. Is Manesty Lane named after a slaver or an abolitionist? Joseph Manesty was the friend and employer of John Newton, the slave trade captain who was later ordained into the Church of England and who wrote the hymns Amazing Grace and Glorious Things of Thee are Spoken. After Newton returned from his third slaving voyage he experienced some sort of fit and was not able to return to sea as a captain. Joseph Manesty secured him a job as a 'tide surveyor' - this job would have involved inspecting ships as they arrived in Liverpool. See also - Great Newton Street.

MANN ISLAND

John Mann was an oil-stone dealer whose premises were on an artificial island created by the construction of George's Dock and Canning Dock. There were two other members of the Mann family who were involved in the slave trade as captains of slave ships Luke and Joseph. Luke was involved in 13 slave voyages between 1764 and 1806 and Joseph was involved in three slave voyages between 1785 and 1788.

ANNE JANE
WHO DIED 17th FEB 1849
AGED [...] YEARS

HANNAH
WHO DIED 11 JANUARY [...]
AGED [...] YEARS

WILLIAM HENRY
WHO DIED 21 DECEMBER 18[...]
AGED [...] YEARS

THE BURIAL PLACE
OF
JOHN MOSS.
BORN FEB. 18. 1782. DIED OCT. 3. 1[...]

MARYLAND STREET

Between 1737 and 1758 Maryland was the ultimate destination of 6 ships from Liverpool carrying kidnapped Africans. It was also a major tobacco growing region and as well as enslaved Africans, the crops were tended by indentured labour and convicted prisoners from Britain. See Hunter Street and Baltimore Street.

MASON STREET

Edward Mason (1735-1814) was a timber merchant and ship builder who built a house in what is now Mason Street. The house and grounds extended the length of Paddington and as far as Smithdown Lane. Mason built the church of St Mary's in Edge Lane entirely at his own expense and was involved in 23 slave voyages between 1764 and 1785.

MOSS STREET

Thomas Moss (????-1805), father of John Moss (1782-1858) of Otterspool owned the land on which this street was built. Thomas Moss was a wealthy merchant and had a share in a lead works in Liverpool. Thomas Moss was involved as part-owner in 23 slave voyages between 1771 and 1805 and was a part-owner with his son in four slave voyages between 1804 and 1805. Upon his death Thomas left £10,000 each to his sons, John, Edward and James and £5,000 to his daughters Margaret and Ellen when they married. His will was later amended to give an additional £10,000 to each of his sons

and £7,000 to his daughters. He left his wife a quarter share of the profit of the lead works having left the business to his sons. John Moss owned plantations worked by enslaved people in the West Indies and received compensation of £40,353 when he was compelled to free the 805 enslaved people on an estate in British Guiana (now Guyana) under the terms of the Slavery Abolition Act, 1833. He was one of the major facilitators behind the Liverpool and Manchester Railway and in 1807 he founded the banking house Moss, Dales & Rogers. He was a man of considerable wealth investing a total of £189,950 in 8 different railway companies. He was also one of four benefactors with slavery connections who paid for St Anne's church in Aigburth Road, Liverpool.

NEW BIRD STREET

Bird Street was named after Alderman Joseph Bird who was Mayor of Liverpool in 1764. The street originally led from James Street to Redcross Street but a change in the layout of the streets meant that it disappeared. New Bird Street was named after Joseph Bird by way of replacement. Bird was involved in 10 slave voyages between 1731 and 1769.

NEWSHAM DRIVE

Newsham Drive takes its name from the Newsham House Estate which was bought by the Council to create a public park. Newsham House was originally built in the late 18th Century by Thomas Molyneaux who was involved as a part-owner in 62 slave voyages between 1778 and 1807. Newsham House is a Grade II Listed Building and was, for a time, known as the Judge's House. Thomas Molyneaux was the business partner of Thomas Leyland - see Walton Hall Park.

OAK HILL PARK

Oak Hill Park is the site of Oak Hill House which was one time home of a number of different people engaged in slavery. Richard Walker (1760-1801), Sir John Tobin (1762-1851) and Richard Watt I (1751-1803) all owned and lived in the house at some stage. Richard Walker was the son-in-law of William James and nephew of Richard Watt I of Jamaica and Speke Hall. William James was a prolific slave trader, he was involved in 132 slave voyages between 1758 and 1776 many of which he carried out as the sole-owner of the slave ship. William James also owned a number of plantations in Jamaica producing sugar and rum by the labour of enslaved people. Sir John Tobin was involved in 15 slave voyages - 6 as a captain and 9 as part-owner of slave ships. Tobin also owned 53 enslaved people in Jamaica. Richard Watt I was a West India merchant with considerable business interests in Liverpool and Jamaica - for more details see Speke Hall Road.

OIL STREET

Oil Street was the site of an oil crushing works owned by a partnership known as Earles & Carter. The firm was founded in October 1798 and the partners were Thomas and William Earle, Thomas Hodgson and John Carter. John Carter did not have any involvement in the slave trade but Thomas and William Earle and Thomas Hodgson were all large scale slave traders. The oil manufactured in Oil Street was linseed oil which was used as a lubricant, an additive to paint and as oil cakes which were fed to cattle. The successful firm was once described as the 'most extensive seed crushers in the country'. Business people who were involved in the slave trade often had other businesses which were complementary to slave trading but this business was completely unrelated.

OLDHAM STREET

Isaac Oldham, a merchant formerly of Redcross Street, built the first house in this street. He was involved in six slave voyages between 1748 and 1758 and was a member of the Liverpool Pilots Committee in 1766.

PARKER STREET

Between 1763 and 1783 Thomas and John Parker were involved in a total of 34 slave voyages. John Parker was, at various times, in partnership with William Davenport, Daniel Backhouse and Thomas Tarleton who, at the time, were among the most significant slave traders in Liverpool. He had premises adjacent to the Old Dock.

PARKFIELD ROAD

Parkfield Road is on of part of the substantial Parkfield House estate which was adjacent to Prince's Park. It was the home of Robert Gladstone Sr. (1773-1835). He was a brother of John Gladstone – see Rodney Street, and Uncle of William Ewart Gladstone. He was in partnership with his brother John as West India merchants and also had a considerable trade in importing cotton from Pernambuco in Brazil. As with West Indies cotton of the time, Brazilian cotton was cultivated by enslaved people. Robert Gladstone was the owner of a plantation in Jamaica on which 468 enslaved people worked. He died before he could receive compensation under the Slavery Abolition Act of 1833. The compensation was passed to his three sons. Robert Gladstone Sr was a director of the Liverpool & Manchester Railway.

PARR STREET

Thomas Parr (1769-1847) had his house on Colquitt Street from 1799 to 1805. The house which remains comprised his home, his counting house and a warehouse complex to the rear. (pictured left) Access to his warehouse was via the street alongside which became known as Parr Street. Between 1744 and 1807 8 members of the Parr family were involved in a total of 145 slave voyages. John and James Parr were also involved in supplying large numbers of muskets as trade goods used by slave traders. John Parr was Mayor of Liverpool 1773/74.

PENKETT ROAD,
WALLASEY

John Penkett was involved as a part-owner in slave ships in 8 slave voyages between 1754 and 1765. He later purchased Liscard Manor House and it's adjacent land in Wallasey, the rural Cheshire side of the Mersey estuary.

PENNY LANE

During the Summer of 2020 and, indeed, for many years previously there has been a debate as to whether or not Penny Lane is named after the Liverpool slave trader James Penny (1741-1799). The debate is, of course, clouded because of the importance in Liverpool popular culture of The Beatles and their song Penny Lane. What is not open to debate is that James Penny Sr and his son, also James, were involved in a total of 62 slave voyages between 1764 and 1807, voyages that would have involved many hundreds of kidnapped Africans being taken from their own countries to be sold as enslaved people in the Americas. Neither is there any debate that James Penny Sr went to London in 1788 to give evidence at the inquiry, launched by the Government, into the slave trade. Penny was convinced that abolition of the slave trade would severely damage the economy of Liverpool and stated as much at the inquiry, saying:

"it would not only greatly affect the commercial interest, but also the landed property of the County of Lancaster and more particularly, the Town of Liverpool; whose fall, in that case, would be as rapid as its rise has been astonishing."

There is considerable evidence that the name "Penny Lane" has its origins elsewhere and there is no evidence to support a link with James Penny.

In June 2020 the International Slavery Museum said that there was "no historical evidence to link Penny Lane to James Penny" and decided to remove Penny Lane from their exhibit of street names that are linked to slave traders. The exhibit has been in place since the museum opened in 2007.

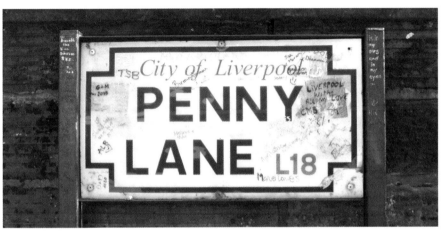

JAMES PENNY SR
(DIED 1799)

In some ways the story of James Penny is a typical one of a number of Liverpool slave traders. He came from Ulverston and after a number successful voyages as captain on a slave ship Penny became a member of a syndicate which carried out slave voyages before leading his own syndicate. Penny was captain of 11 successful slave voyages from Liverpool, sailing ships predominately owned by Miles Barber who became a prolific Liverpool slave trader. Barber had already initiated voyages from Lancaster which is, probably, where Penny knew him from. Slave trading was a high risk business and for an owner to have a knowledgeable and reliable captain who knew the trade would have been a great advantage. The 11 successful slave voyages would have made Penny a moderately wealthy man.

When Penny started to carry out voyages in his own name his syndicate included men from his home town – Moses Benson, John Backhouse and Thomas Dixon, all of whom would go on to be major slave traders in Liverpool.

Of the 53 voyages which Penny was involved in as captain or part-owner, 40 of them were completed successfully with the other 13 falling victim to shipwreck or capture by French privateers.

Arguably Penny's biggest contribution to the Liverpool slave trade was his inclusion, in 1788, with John Tarleton, Robert Norris, John Matthews and Archibald Dalzell in a delegation to London to argue in Parliament in favour of continuing the African slave trade. For their efforts Penny and his colleagues were given the Freedom of Liverpool and Penny was presented with a fine piece of silverware which is currently on display in the International Slavery Museum.

Penny had carried out his obligations to Liverpool and had been rewarded. Had a street been named after him, it would have been in the city centre not in a semi-rural area with which he had no connection.

POWNALL SQUARE/POWNALL STREET

William Pownall Sr (1718-1767) was involved as a part-owner of slave ships in 39 slave voyages. He was Mayor of Liverpool in 1767 and was a benefactor of the now demolished St Thomas's Church in Liverpool city centre. His name is recorded on an interpretation board on the site of the former church in which he is described as a "successful merchant, magistrate and shipbuilder". His involvement in the slave trade is not mentioned. It is widely reputed that William Pownall died after catching a chill while trying, in his role as a magistrate, to quell a riot in Salthouse Dock in 1767 - the year of his Mayoralty. See also Tabley Street.

RAINFORD SQUARE

The Rainford family were substantial West India merchants who were involved with the Blundells in trade with Jamaica. Peter Rainford was an Alderman, a Justice of the Peace for Liverpool and Mayor of Liverpool in 1741.

RATHBONE STREET

Rathbones, the business which started in 1742 and still survives in 2020 in Liverpool and London, set great store by their strong opposition to the slave trade and slavery and yet closer examination of the company's own publications reveal that this is not entirely accurate.

It is certainly true that William Rathbone III (1726-1789) and William Rathbone IV (1749-1802) were both members of the Liverpool Committee for the Abolition of the Slave Trade. There is considerable truth in the claims made by the family; in her 1992 book Rathbone Brothers: From Merchant to Banker, 1742-1992, Lucie Nottingham writes "William Rathbone IV continued to work for abolition, and the firm took a determined stance, refusing to have any part in the slave trade or, indeed, to sell timber or vessels for use in the trade …". William Rathbone III, who was primarily a timber merchant, did not become involved in any slave voyages nor did he sell timber to be used for building slaving ships, although he had no qualms about buying mahogany from Barbados and Jamaica which was, of course, cultivated by enslaved people – this labour being the very reason for the slave trade in the first place.

William Rathbone III expanded the trade carried out by the company to include sugar, coffee, tobacco, ginger and, of course, cotton, all products cultivated by enslaved people. Indeed, the first cotton imported into Liverpool was done so by Rathbones. The reason behind buying goods cultivated by enslaved people were entirely financial since they were significantly cheaper. The 1913 book, edited by Eleanor Rathbone entitled "Records of the Rathbone Family", states "A plantation thus worked [with slave or convict labour] could produce, taking raw sugar at 3d [1.5p]. a lb. [454 grams], £37:10s [£37.5]). per acre [0.404 hectares]. When refined and sold in London or Liverpool at 12d.[5p] a lb.[454 grams], the £37:10s [£37.50]. became £150."

William Rathbone III also bought a kidnapped African in Liverpool - a 14 year old boy called Tom. While it *may* have happened in Liverpool, the writer has not been able to find records of any other similar instances among slave traders in Liverpool. Rathbone sent Tom to a friend in Germany by way of a "present". Tom would not, of course, have been a slave and would have worked as a servant in the house of William Rathbone's friend. The fact remains that the boy had been kidnapped from his home in Africa and separated from his family before being brought to a completely alien culture only to be treated as a "commodity". William Rathbone III paid £31 10s [£31.50] for Tom although the full cost of the 'transaction', including commission and shipping expenses, was £32 12s 1d [£32.60]. In his 2008 book David Lascelles "The Story of the Rathbones since 1742" says of this matter 'It might not have been quite as odious as packing dozens of unclothed Africans off to America in shackles, but it was traffic in human beings nonetheless.'

"

The past has a disconcerting habit of bursting, uninvited and unwelcome into the present

"

- David Olusoga
Writing in the Observer on 12th July 2015

RENSHAW STREET

John Renshaw died in 1805 at the age of 83, his son, Rev. S. Renshaw, was one time Rector of Liverpool. John Renshaw was involved in 6 slave voyages between 1757 and 1763.

ST. PAUL'S CHURCH.

RIGBY STREET

Gilbert Rigby lived on the corner of Old Hall Street and what was to become Rigby Street. He was part-owner of slave ships involved in 16 voyages between 1759 and 1768. He died in 1769 and was buried in St Paul's churchyard. Another member of the Rigby family, Peter, was an iron monger who was involved in 40 slave voyages between 1760 and 1795. Peter Rigby built Moss House in 1776 and was Mayor of Liverpool in 1774.

RODNEY STREET

Rodney Street is named after Admiral George Brydges, 1st Baron Rodney. He had a long, if somewhat controversial naval career, but succeeded, at the 1782 Battle of the Saintes,

in defeating the French, saving Jamaica and securing the West Indies which were of such importance to the traders and merchants of Liverpool. Rodney Street became a fashionable place to live because it was away from noise and smells of the town yet close enough for merchants to get to their counting houses easily. Many people linked with slavery lived in Rodney Street but perhaps the most famous was John Gladstone (1764-1851) who had a house built there at the cost of £1,570 in 1793. John Gladstone was one of a large number of people drawn by the growth of city who moved to Liverpool. He was from Scotland as were many others as well as a number coming from Lancaster and South Cumbria. For the first 15 years of his time in Liverpool, John Gladstone was involved in the grain trade which made him very wealthy. He subsequently diversified to trade with Calcutta (now Kolkata) India and dealt in tobacco from Virginia as well as various goods from the West Indies. In 1802 he was involved in one slave voyage when 395 kidnapped Africans were transported from Bonny in West Africa to the Bahamas. This one slave voyage and John Gladstone's involvement in importing goods cultivated by enslaved people were not his only involvement in slavery.

He owned a number of plantations he owned in Jamaica and British Guiana (now Guyana) and, under the 1833 Slavery Abolition Act, he received compensation of over £112,716 in respect of 2,912 enslaved Africans who he was forced to release from slavery. He became an MP (Lancaster 1818-20; Woodstock 1820-26 & Berwick-upon-Tweed 1826-27) and was made a baronet in 1851. Three of Gladstone's sons also became Members of Parliament most

notably William Ewart Gladstone (1809-1898) who was born at 62 Rodney Street (pictured above) and was four times both Chancellor of the Exchequer and Prime Minister. William Ewart Gladstone was a Liberal although his views on slavery, doubtless moulded by those of his father, were far from what we would think of as 'Liberal' now and in June 2020 the University of Liverpool announced that they are removing his name from one of their student accommodation blocks. John Gladstone, in association with other Scots in Liverpool, paid

for the construction of a Scottish chapel in Oldham Street, Liverpool. They also funded the Caledonian School which faced it where Liverpool's leading Scottish families sent their children to be educated. In 1815 Gladstone paid for the construction of St Thomas's Anglican Church in Seaforth and St Andrew's Episcopal Church in Renshaw Street. The latter had a school for educating poor children. John Gladstone used some of his considerable wealth to buy property in Liverpool, London and Scotland. He bought Seaforth House - 1811; 5 Grafton St London - 1818; Balbegno Castle in Kincardineshire - 1819; Balbegno House also in Kincardineshire - 1830 for £80,000; Phesdo House in Aberdeenshire - 1844 for £32,000. Fasque Estate, Fettercairne, Aberdeenshire and Stockwell Lodge, Surrey. At the time of his death in 1851 he was worth £636,000 at a time when a labourer in Liverpool was earning less than £50 a year.

RODNEY STREET'S OTHER LINKS WITH SLAVERY

2 Rodney Street
Home of Lister Ellis (1778-1829)

Ellis was an owner of enslaved people on a plantation he owned in British Guiana (now Guyana). He was a West India merchant in the Liverpool firm of Charles, William and Francis Shand as well as a cotton spinner with a mill in Keighley, Yorkshire. Lister Ellis is buried at St George's Church, Everton.

10 Rodney Street
Alexander Hoyes (1801-1875)

An owner of enslaved people on 3 plantations in Jamaica lived at 10 Rodney Street. Hoyes received over £3,684 when he was obliged to free his enslaved workers by the Slavery Abolition Act of 1833.

16 Rodney Street
John Hayward Turner (1789-1872)

Of Abercromby Square and later 16 Rodney Street was a partner in the Liverpool cotton broking firm of Salisbury, Turner and Earle. The other partners were Nicholas Salisbury and Hardman Earle. Under the terms of the Slavery Abolition Act of 1833 Turner received compensation in excess of £19,600 after being compelled to free the 1,358 enslaved people who worked on his plantations in Antigua.

19 Rodney Street
Place of death of William Peterswald (????-1847)

William Peterswald had been a planter in Jamaica before he returned first to Edinburgh where his wife's family was from then to Liverpool. He received compensation of £4,098 in respect of 200 enslaved Africans on a plantation he owned in Jamaica. William Peterswald's will left money for his wife, Jane, and his son, William, but if William was to die then one half of the residue was to go to his children of colour by Hellen Cunningham in Jamaica.

61 Rodney Street
Home of Daniel Willink (1780-1859)

A Liverpool merchant and Consul for the Netherlands in the port. His office was at 3 Goree Piazza in Liverpool. Upon the emancipation of enslaved people in the British Empire Willink received compensation of £13,378 in respect of 266 enslaved people who worked his plantation in Demerara (now part of Guyana). Like many other people who received compensation for freeing enslaved people Willink was a considerable investor in the new railway companies which were starting around the same time, investing a total of £38,750 in a total of 12 companies.

ROE STREET

William Roe was a copper smelter who opened a works on the shore of Toxteth Park in 1767. Copper was much in demand as plating for ship's hulls and, in the form of manillas (pictured), as trade goods in the slave trade. His business would have brought William Roe into contact with slave traders. Between 1769 and 1786 he was involved as a part owner of ships involved in six slave voyages.

Manillas were labelled as "Copper Nails" on ships' manifests but are much too small to be worn as jewellery.

ROSCOE LANE/ROSCOE STREET

William Roscoe (1753-1831) was a staunch abolitionist, of this there can be no doubt, although his abolitionist credentials do require some further examination. Having worked for a bookseller, Roscoe trained as a lawyer and from 1774 to 1797 Roscoe was an attorney in partnership with Aspinall and Hall.

In 1792 Roscoe went into business in an attempt to reclaim Chat Moss and Trafford Moss with Thomas Wakefield, who was a Liverpool sugar refiner. Wakefield had participated in at least one slave voyage and had other links to the slave trade – see Highfield Road. When William Clarkes bank was in financial difficulties in 1793, Roscoe was called in as an attorney to assist and, at the insistence of Sir Benjamin Hammet of Esdail, William Clarke's London agents, Roscoe was asked to join the partnership. In 1802 William Roscoe expanded the partnership of the bank, by now known as Clarke, Roscoe & Co by admitting Thomas Leyland as senior partner to form Leyland, Clarkes & Roscoe. Thomas Leyland was a significant participant in the trans-Atlantic slave trade being involved in over 70 slave voyages, a number of which occured at the same time that he was in partnership with Roscoe. The banking partnership was dissolved by mutual agreement on 31st December 1806. It has been suggested that this break-up was caused by Roscoe's support for abolition. This is not really credible because both Roscoe and Leyland would be very aware of each other's views on slavery before the partnership was created. As partners, the business would have been worked on the basis of 'joint and several liability' whereby all the partners were responsible as individuals for the total debts of the business. It is more likely that Leyland joined the firm to give it additional financial strength and left again once he had learned how to operate a bank. Leyland started his own bank, Leyland and Bullins, on 10th January, 1807.

While undoubtedly a strong supporter of abolition, Roscoe's election as a Member of Parliament for Liverpool in 1806 poses more questions about his commitment to this cause. Roscoe was proposed for Parliament by Thomas Earle and seconded by Thomas Leyland who were among the most prolific and successful slave traders in Liverpool and men who had plenty of money to fight the election, including funding the necessary bribery which was common in elections at the time. The expenses figures for the election bear this out – General Gascoyne and his supporters spent £3,000, General Tarleton and his supporters spent £4,000 but Roscoe and his supporters spent £12,000. Earle and Leyland were hard-headed businessmen and would have been seeking a return on their "investment" in getting Roscoe elected. Roscoe started to repay this "investment" straight away. At a public dinner held at the Golden Lion in Dale St to celebrate his election his speech included the following:

"It has been the fashion throughout the Kingdom to regard the town of Liverpool and its inhabitants in an unfavourable light on account of the share it has in this [African] trade. But I will venture to say that this idea is founded on ignorance, and I will here assert, as I always shall, that men more independent, of greater virtue and private worth , than the merchants of Liverpool do not exist in any part of these kingdoms. The African trade is the trade of the nation, not of any particular place; it is a trade, till lately, sanctioned by Parliament and long continued under the authority of the Government. I do not make this remark in vindication of the character of any gentlemen engaged in the trade, who stand in need of none, but in order to shew that if any loss should arise to any individuals who are concerned in it, it is incumbent upon Government to make them a full compensation for the losses they may so sustain."

[Emphasis by the author.] (See: Williams, G; History of the Liverpool Privateers and Letters of Marque with an Account of the Liverpool Slave Trade 1744 – 1812; McGill-Queen's University Press 2004. P.595.)

While he continued to voice his opposition to the slave trade in Parliament, Roscoe also spoke up for those in Liverpool involved in the trade:

"Mr Roscoe declared, that, after having performed the great duty of abolishing the Slave Trade, which had so disgraced the land, he thought the house bound to consider the situation of those who should suffer from the annihilation of a system so long sanctioned by the Legislature."
(See Hansard: Slave Trade Abolition Bill – 20th February, 1807.)

Three days later Roscoe renewed his request for compensation for slave traders and added an appeal for the removal of the monopoly of the East-India Company on trade with India:

"… He did not think he should discharge his duty to his constituents if he did not urge the claim the West-India merchants had on the public for compensation. … He thought that our East-India possessions were inseparable from the interests of Great Britain, as a free and independent nation, but there ought to be no exclusive trade in the East-India company. The trade of India ought to be thrown open to the whole body of British merchants."
(See Hansard: Slave Trade Abolition Bill – 23rd February, 1807.)

William Roscoe was MP for Liverpool for 6 months from 1806 to 1807 which meant that he was able to vote for the abolition of the slave trade. He was not an MP for long because there was another General Election in 1807. He stood for election again in 1807 although, without the financial backing of Leyland and Earle, he was not successful.

ST DOMINGO ROAD AND ST DOMINGO VALE

St Domingo was the name given to land and a house constructed by George Campbell who was a West India merchant. As well as being a sugar merchant George Campbell and his son, George Jr, were involved as captain, part-owner and owners of a number of slave ships which completed 40 voyages between 1736 and 1769. In common with many slave ship owners, George Campbell bought Letters of Marque which made his ships privateers with permission to attack any ship of a country that Britain was at war with. It was not uncommon for ships engaged in carrying people from Africa to the Americas to have a Letter of Marque, neither was it unusual for slave traders to arm some of the Africans they were carrying in order to assist in the fight with ships being attacked or to help defend their ship from privateers from other countries. The name St Domingo comes from ships originating from the port of St Domingo which were captured by George Campbell's ships. St Domingo was George Campbell's country house and he also had a town house in Duke Street.

SEEL STREET

Between 1715 and 1758 Thomas Seel Sr and his son Thomas Jr were involved in a total of 24 slave voyages. This involvement in the slave trade came as a direct result of Thomas Seel Sr's involvement in the tobacco business. Seel would import tobacco into Liverpool and export manufactured goods. Thomas Seel's early slave voyages were directly linked to a need for labourers in Rappahannock, Virginia from where he was buying tobacco. In the course of 7 voyages to the area Seel's ships carried 747 kidnapped Africans who were sold into slavery. Thomas Seel lived in a large house with a substantial garden which fronted onto Hanover Street but extended a long way back up what is, since 1790, Seel Street. Under the 1826 Bank Charter Street, the Bank of England was allowed to open branches outside London. Liverpool was among the early sites chosen for a branch. The Bank of England bought Thomas Seel's house from the family and used it as their first branch in Liverpool. For many years there was an interpretation board, showing Seel's house and garden, fixed to the wall of the Hanover Street Tesco store which faced Seel Street. As a direct result of the debate initiated over the legacy of the slave trade in various cities the board was removed by the property owner Liverpool One in June 2020.

SIR THOMAS STREET

Sir Thomas Street in Liverpool city centre is named after Sir Thomas Johnson 1664 – 1728. Johnson's father, also called Thomas, was Mayor of Liverpool in 1670, he was a tobacco and sugar trader and amassed a fortune from the exploitative labour of enslaved people in the Americas. This fortune passed to his son, Thomas Jr, who is claimed by many to be responsible for the foundation of Liverpool as we now know it. Thomas Johnson Jr does have a good claim to this accolade, having been Mayor of Liverpool in 1695 and Member of Parliament for Liverpool from 1701 to 1723. He was responsible for separation of the parish of Liverpool from the parish of Walton-on-the-Hill which gave Liverpool and Walton separate identities. Perhaps most importantly for the future of Liverpool it was Johnson who was the driving force behind the construction of what is now known as the Old Dock, which was opened in 1715. The now demolished churches of St Peter's and St George's were also built through his efforts. He was knighted in 1708. There is, however, another side to Johnson which is less attractive. Retaining his late father's business interest in sugar and tobacco meant that he was involved in the trade of goods cultivated by enslaved people. Between the years of 1700 and 1717 he engaged in four slave voyages as well as being responsible for transporting 639 Jacobite prisoners to Virginia, where they would work for him without pay for seven years. The government paid Sir Thomas 40s ($£2$) per prisoner to transport them. Tobacco importers were allowed to deposit bonds as security for the duty payable by them on tobacco which was for domestic use. Johnson was often in financial difficulties, as his business involved him tying up large sums of capital on a speculative basis and, in 1717, he and his son in law/business partner, Richard Gildart – see Gildart Street, - owed over £7,820 to the Crown in unpaid duty on tobacco. In 1728 Johnson resigned his seat in Parliament and took up the post of collector of customs in Virginia leaving Richard Gildart to deal with his debts.

SLATER STREET

Slater street is named after Gill (Gilbert) Slater who took part in 48 slave voyages between 1759 and 1793. Slater went bankrupt in 1793 in the general financial crisis that marked the beginning of the wars with revolutionary France, which would later become known as the Napoleonic Wars.

SPARLING STREET

Between 1768 and 1794, John Sparling was involved in 26 slave voyages and his son, John Jr, was involved in another 6. Sparling was in partnership with William Bolden and were tobacco merchants in Liverpool. Both Sparling and Bolden were partners in the John Lawrence & Co of Norfolk, Virginia and John Sparling was a partner in Sparling, Lawrence & Co of Suffolk, Virginia. John's younger brother, George, was the manager of the business in Suffolk, Virginia and owned 25% of the shares. He retired in 1796 and bought the St Domingo estate – see St Domingo Vale. Sparling demolished the house built by George Campbell and built a fine mansion on the site. John Sparling was Mayor of Liverpool 1790/91.

SPEKE HALL ROAD

Speke Hall has a number of connections with slavery. Richard Norris (1670-1730) was the 6th son of Thomas Norris of Speke, he was a freeman of Liverpool from 1693, bailiff 1695/6, a member of the Common Council from 1695 until his death in 1730, deputy Mayor in 1707 and Mayor 1700/01 and sheriff of Lancashire 1718/19. He amassed a fortune in trading in tobacco and sugar and was involved in three slave voyages between 1700 and 1723. Norris inherited Speke Hall from his brother in 1726.

The most notable connections which Speke Hall has with slavery come via the Watt family. Richard Watt III – 1786–1855 was a slave owner. He was son of Richard Watt II (d. 1803) and great-nephew and heir of Richard Watt I (1724-1796) who had bought Speke Hall in November 1795 for £73,000 (although he never lived there) and Bishop Burton estates in Yorkshire after his return from Jamaica. Richard Watt I lived in Jamaica for a number of years trading as a "slave factor" and owning a plantation cultivated by enslaved people. As well as trading extensively in 'slave grown goods' he was also involved in two slave voyages in partnership with Richard Savage, one in 1760 and the other in 1767.

In 1793, he bought another ship in his own name and used it to transport 549 kidnapped Africans to Jamaica where they were sold into slavery. Ten Africans died on this first voyage and on its second voyage the ship was captured by a French privateer.

Richard Watt I was a trustee of the Blue Coat Hospital, a governor and trustee of the Liverpool Infirmary and dispensary and a founder member and trustee of the Old Swan Charity School.

The Bishop's throne in Liverpool Cathedral was paid for by a donation from the Watt family and carries the inscription "In memory of Richard Watt, citizen of Liverpool 1724 – 1796". (pictured opposite bottom right)

Richard Watt III had been born in Liverpool and baptised in St Thomas's church although he grew up in Yorkshire. He inherited sufficient money not to need to have a profession and his wealth was increased by compensation of £4,485 under the Slavery Abolition Act, 1833 in respect of 256 enslaved people on an estate in Jamaica which he owned. Richard Watt III had inherited George's Plain in Westmoreland Jamaica as well as Speke Hall under the will of Richard Watt I.

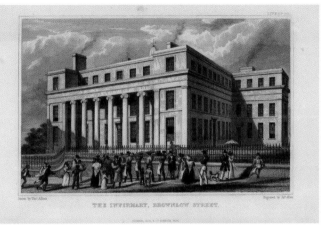

THE INFIRMARY, BROWNLOW STREET.

SPEKELAND ROAD

Spekeland House was built by Thomas Earle. Spekelands, Smeatham Lane was the home, in 1807, of Thomas Earle, Merchant. Thomas and his father, also Thomas, participated in 82 slave voyages between 1767 and 1804. Thomas was partner of William Earle in Thomas & William Earle and Co who had their counting house at 51 Hanover Street, Liverpool. T & W Earle & Co were West India merchants. The Earle family were very deeply involved in many aspects of slavery over many years. See also Earle Street/Earle Road and Oil Street.

SPRINGWOOD AVENUE

Springwood House was built by William Shand (1784-1848) although it was completed by Sir Thomas Brocklebank the ship owner. Shand was a West India merchant who was in partnership with his brother Charles and his nephew William Shand. William Shand was the recipient of a considerable amount of compensation under the Slavery Abolition Act, 1833 in respect of estates of which he was either owner or mortgagee in Antigua. William Shand received in excess of £62,627 in respect of 2,335 enslaved Africans.

TABLEY STREET

William Pownall, who was Mayor in 1767, came from Tabley. He was involved in 43 slave voyages between 1753 and 1770. See also Pownall Square.

TARLETON STREET

Between 1740 and 1799 just 4 members of the Tarleton family were involved in over 150 slave voyages. Thomas Tarleton owned a plantation in Grenada which he had inherited from his father John. The Tarleton family were significant dealers in goods cultivated by enslaved people. Although he was never directly involved in any slave voyages, one member of the Tarleton family, Banastre (later Sir Banastre) Tarleton, was MP for Liverpool from 1790 to 1806 and from 1807 to 1812. During his time as an MP Banastre Tarleton spoke against and voted against the abolition of the slave trade. John Tarleton was Mayor of Liverpool 1764/65. Clayton Tarleton was Mayor of Liverpool 1792/93.

See also - Aigburth Hall Road.

TOBIN STREET, WALLASEY

John (later Sir John) Tobin (1762-1851) was involved in 15 slave voyages, 6 as a captain and 9 as a co-owner of slaving ships between 1794 and 1804. He married Sarah Aspinall in 1798, the daughter of James Aspinall, a member of a prolific slave trading family.

In common with many slave traders Tobin also had other business interests. He was a partner in Hughes and Tobin, ship owners; Tobin & Co insurance brokers and the Union Mill Company who were rope makers. He received over £1,030 in compensation under the Slavery Abolition Act, 1833 in respect of 53 enslaved Africans in Jamaica and was a pioneer of the West African palm oil business - at the time palm oil was cultivated by enslaved people. John Tobin also owned a gunpowder mill in Ireland which supplied gunpowder to others trading with West Africa considerably beyond 1807 when Britain and a number of other countries had made the slave trade illegal.

Owner of various pieces of land in Wallasey (at that time part of Cheshire), he built Liscard Hall, Wallasey in 1835 having built Liscard House, Wallasey in 1833 for his son who was vicar of St John's Church in Egremont, Wallasey. The Church was built between 1832 - 1833 and the land was given by John Tobin along with £1,000 towards the building cost. Liscard House is no longer standing and only the stables of Liscard Hall remain. However, the church is still in existence although redundant - it is Listed Grade II. Before moving to Wallasey, John Tobin had lived at Oakhill House, Old Swan, Liverpool and was Mayor of Liverpool 1819/20. He was knighted in 1820.

VIRGINIA STREET

Tobacco was an important import into Liverpool and much of it came from the Maryland/Virginia area of what were initially the American colonies and later part of the United States of America. The tobacco that came into Liverpool from America up to the 1860s was cultivated by enslaved Africans.

WALTON HALL AVENUE

Walton Hall was the home of Thomas Leyland (1752-1827). Thomas Leyland was originally a merchant who diversified into ship owning and banking. He earned the nickname "Lucky Leyland" after jointly winning a lottery prize of £20,000 with his business partner. Leyland expanded his existing trading activities and also moved into slave trading. Slave trading proved to be very profitable for him. For example, his ship "Enterprize" made a voyage to Africa and then on to Havana in Cuba in 1803/4. This voyage was one of a number made by the same vessel over a number of years. It cost Leyland and his partners Thomas Molyneaux and Richard Bullin (Leyland's nephew) £17,045 to fit out and purchase trade goods. Upon arrival in Havana the ship was carrying 412 Eboe people from Africa - 194 men, 32 men-boys, 66 boys, 42 women, 36 women-girls and 42 girls. Upon sale of the enslaved people, and allowing for the profit on goods shipped from Havana to Liverpool, there was a profit of £24,430 to be shared between the partners in the voyage. Leyland's share of the profits was £12,215 against his share of the costs of £8,522 - a profit of 143%. At the time a labourer in Liverpool would do well to earn 3 shillings (15p) per day/90p per week. In 1802 Thomas Leyland became a partner in a bank with Clarke and Roscoe, an unlikely business partnership given William Roscoe's abolitionist credentials. Leyland left this banking partnership at the end of 1806 and started his own bank, Leyland & Co, on 1st January 1807. From 1809 the Bank was known as Leyland & Bullins. It merged, in 1901, with the North and South Wales Bank, which subsequently became part of the Midland Bank, which is now part of HSBC. The former Head Office of Leyland and Bullins Bank can be found on the corner of Castle Street and Brunswick St. Thomas Leyland's town house was in Duke Street and his warehouse and the first premises for his bank were in York Street, off Duke St. He was a member of Liverpool Chamber of Commerce and was Mayor of Liverpool three times - 1798/99, 1814/15 and 1820/21. When Thomas Leyland died in 1827 he left cash and stocks in excess of £736,000, this amount has led to him being referred to as the richest person who has ever lived in Liverpool.

Top left – Leyland and Bullins Bank Head Office, Castle Street.
Bottom Right – Thomas Leyland's original warehouse, counting house and bank, York Street off Duke Street.

WILBERFORCE HOUSE/ GOREE PIAZZA

Wilberforce House and Goree Piazza are names that are no longer found on maps of Liverpool. Both the building and the piazza were named after the slavery abolitionist William Wilberforce (1759-1833). When a large office block was built in 1967/67 close to the site of the Goree warehouses, which had been demolished in 1959, it was named Wilberforce House as a direct contradiction of the slavery connotations of the building that had recently been demolished.

After the building and plaza were completed, Merseyside Civic Society commissioned a fountain so go in the centre of the plaza. The result was Richard Huws's so called "bucket fountain" (pictured). There are two viewing towers adjacent to the fountain and one has a copper interpretation board which tells the story of the Goree warehouses. The board has been dirty for some years and, as of 2019, the bucket fountain itself is under threat because the building owners are seeking to enlarge their development. The building and the piazza no longer serve to remind us of William Wilberforce and are now called Beetham Plaza as a reminder of the company that developed the site in 2003.

WILBERFORCE ROAD

While the name Wilberforce has disappeared from Liverpool city centre it is still remembered in a road in Walton. The road was named in the far more recent past than others in this book and honours the name of William Wilberforce (1759-1833) who was leader of the movement to abolish the slave trade in the United Kingdom. Wilberforce was MP for Kingston-Upon-Hull from 1780 to 1784, Yorkshire 1784 to 1812 and Bramber 1812 to 1825. Wilberforce died just three days after hearing that the passage of the Slavery Abolition Act, 1833 through Parliament was assured.

This Act abolished slavery throughout the British Empire with the exception of lands controlled by the East India Company, Ceylon (now Sri Lanka) and St Helena. The Slavery Abolition Act, 1833 did not, however, provide for the immediate emancipation of enslaved people, other than those under the age of 6. Enslaved people over the age of 6 were referred to as "apprentices" instead of "slaves" and their servitude would extend to 1st August 1838 or, in some cases, 1st August 1840. There was widespread objection to this and full emancipation to all was granted before 1838. The Act provided for compensation paid by the British government not to those who had been enslaved but, instead, to those who had enslaved them. The total amount of compensation was set at £20 million which represented 40% of annual income of the UK Treasury at the time or 5% of the UK's Gross Domestic Product. In order to fund the compensation the government had to borrow £15 million which it did by issuing undated gilts. These gilts were only repaid in 2015 when the government redeemed all the remaining undated gilts.

SLAVE EMANCIPATION; OR, JOHN BULL GULLED OUT OF TWENTY MILLIONS.

Printed and Published by G. Drake, 12, Houghton Street, Clare Market.

WILLIAM BROWN STREET

William (later Sir William) Brown (1784-1864) was a major philanthropist in Liverpool giving to many good causes. He paid for the Library and Museum in the street which now bears his name and yet William Brown acquired at least part of his considerable wealth from the importation of cotton from the southern states of America. At one time it was calculated that W & J Brown in Liverpool were importing 75% of all American cotton that came to the United Kingdom and it was not unusual for the firm to handle 30,000 bales of cotton in one transaction.

Although it is generally accepted that William Brown came to Liverpool in either 1809 or 1810 there is an intriguing reference in a privately published history of Brown Shipley, the bank he created, from 1960 that William Brown was involved in a slave voyage.

Speaking of William Brown's banking arrangements in Liverpool, Aytoun Ellis writes
"William Brown appears to have transferred his account, in a short while, to Leyland & Bullins. Thomas Leyland, like [John] Moss, was a shipowner engaged in the Africa trade. He was Liverpool's leading merchant and Mayor at that time. Apparently William Brown unwittingly joined him in one enterprise concerned with the slave trade – a very lucrative venture – but when realising too late the nature of the "adventure" he promptly withdrew his account."
(See Ellis, A; Heir of Adventure The story of Brown, Shipley & Co. Merchant Bankers 1810 1960; published privately by Brown Shipley & Co. Page 44.)

The dates here are interesting. A William Brown is shown as a partner with Thomas Leyland in a slave voyage in 1807 yet the earliest suggested date for William Brown coming to Liverpool is 1809. Add to this that Thomas Leyland was Mayor of Liverpool three times – 1798/99, 1814/15 and 1820/21 and the fact that although Thomas Leyland formed his bank on 1st January 1807, it did not become Leyland & Bullins until 1809. The reference in Brown Shipley's own book suggests a slave voyage in 1814 or 1815 some 7 or 8 years after the trans-Atlantic slave trade became illegal. William Brown was not in Liverpool in 1798/99 and, by 1820/21 he was already very well established.

In 1846 he was elected, unopposed, as Liberal MP for South Lancashire. In 1859 he raised and equipped, at his own expense, the 1st Brigade Lancashire Artillery Volunteers. As an artillery unit the expense of raising it would have been very considerable.

In 1863 he became 1st Baron Richmond Hill - this was Richmond Hill in Everton which had been his home for many years.

"… an important part of the city's history which has for too long been rejected, forgotten or ignored.

- A Tibbles
Liverpool and the Slave Trade;
Liverpool University Press, 2018

Bibliography and Further reading:

Ascott, D.E., Lewis, F., Power, M.; Liverpool 1660-1750 People, Prosperity and Power; Liverpool University Press,2006

Baines, E; History, Directory, and Gazetteer of the County Palatine of Lancaster, Vol I; Wm Wales & Co, 1824.

Baines, T; History of the Commerce and Town of Liverpool; Longman, Brown, Green and Longmans, London, 1852

Bennett, R.J.; The Voice of Liverpool Business: The First Chamber of Commerce and the Atlantic Economy 1774-c.1796; Liverpool Chamber of Commerce, 2010

Brooke, R; Liverpool as it was 1775 to 1800; first published 1853; Liverpool Libraries and Information Services, 2003

Checkland, S; The Gladstones A Family Biography 1764-1851; Cambridge University Press, 1971

Crow, H; The Memoires of Captain Hugh Crow – The Life and Times of a Slave Trade Captain; Bodleian Library, Oxford 2007 (Originally published 1830)

Dawes, M & Ward-Perkins; Country Banks of England and Wales, Private Provincial Banks & Bankers 1688-1953; The Chartered Institute of Bankers, 2000

Duggan, M; Sugar for the House A History of Early Sugar Refining in North West England; Fonthill Media Ltd, 2013

Earle, P; The Earles of Liverpool A Georgian Merchant Dynasty; Liverpool University Press, 2015

Ellis, A; Heir of Adventure, The Story of Brown, Shipley & Co. Merchant Bankers 1810 1960; Privately published Brown, Shipley & Co Ltd, London, 1960

Ellison, T; The Cotton Trade of Great Britain: Including a history of the Liverpool Cotton Market and of the Liverpool Cotton Brokers' Association; Effingham Wilson, London, 1886

Enfield, W; History of Liverpool 1773; Warrington, 1773; Republished 2019 The Dusty Teapot Company

Gifford, Lord, Brown, W, Bundey, R; Loosen the Shackles; Karia Press London, 1989

Haggerty, S; 'Merely for Money'? Business Culture in the British Atlantic, 1750-1815; Liverpool University Press, 2012.

Haggerty, S; Webster, A; White, N.J.; eds. The Empire in one City? Liverpool's inconvenient past; Manchester University Press, 2008.

Hughes, J.; Liverpool Banks and Bankers 1760-1837; Henry Young & Sons, Liverpool, 1906

Lascelles, D.; The Story of Rathbones Since 1742; Privately published, Rathbone Brothers plc, London, 2008

Lloyd-Jones, T; Liverpool Street Names; The Bluecoat Press, Liverpool 1992

Morgan, K; Liverpool's Dominance in the British Slave Trade, 1740-1807; Richardson, D; Schwarz, S & Tibbles, A – eds; Liverpool and Transatlantic Slavery; Liverpool University Press, 2010.

Nottingham, L.; Rathbone Brothers From Merchant to Banker 1742-`1992; Rathbone Brothers, 1992.

Picton, J; Memorials of Liverpool; Longmans, Green & Co, London, 1875

Rathbone, E; Ed.; Records of the Rathbone Family; Private publication, Edinburgh, 1913.

Richardson, D, Schwarz, S, Tibbles, A, Eds; Liverpool and Transatlantic Slavery; Liverpool University Press, 2007.

Thomas, H.; The Slave Trade – the History of the Atlantic Slave Trade 1440-1870 Picador, 1997.

Troughton; The History of Liverpool 1810; William Robinson, Liverpool, 1810; republished by The Dusty Teapot 2019

Trust, G; John Moss of Otterspool (1782-1858) Railway Pioneer – Slave Owner – Banker; Author House UK Ltd, 2011

Williams, G; History of the Liverpool Privateers and Letters of Marque with an account of the Liverpool Slave Trade 1744-1812; first published 1897; Liverpool University Press, 2004

Slavery resources on line:

For details of Slave Voyages: https://www.slavevoyages.org/

For details of the Legacies of British Slave-ownership: https://www.ucl.ac.uk/lbs/